Additional praise for
STILLNESS IS THE KEY

"Some authors give advice. Ryan Holiday distills wisdom. This book is a must read." —CAL NEWPORT, *NEW YORK TIMES* BESTSELLING AUTHOR OF *DIGITAL MINIMALISM*

"Don't be fooled. Within the pages of this unassuming little book lie a life-changing idea: that in order to move forward, we must learn to be still. Ryan Holiday has done it again." —SOPHIA AMORUSO, COFOUNDER AND CEO, GIRLBOSS

"In the world today the dangers are many—most notably, the endless distractions and petty battles that make us act without purpose or direction. In this book, through his masterful synthesis of Eastern and Western philosophy, Ryan Holiday teaches us all how to maintain our focus and presence of mind amid the sometimes overwhelming conflicts and troubles of twenty-first-century life." —ROBERT GREENE, *NEW YORK TIMES* BESTSELLING AUTHOR OF *THE 48 LAWS OF POWER*

"Ryan Holiday is one of the brilliant writers and minds of our time. In *Stillness Is the Key* he gives us the blueprint to clear our minds, recharge our souls, and reclaim our power." —JON GORDON, BESTSELLING AUTHOR OF *THE ENERGY BUS*

"Ryan Holiday is a national treasure and a master in the field of self-mastery. In his most compelling book yet, he has mined both the classical literature of the ancient world and cultural touchstones from Mister Rogers to Tiger Woods, and brought his learnings to us in terms that the frantic, distracted, overcaffeinated modern mind can understand and put to use. Highly recommended." —STEVEN PRESSFIELD, BESTSELLING AUTHOR OF *THE WAR OF ART* AND *THE ARTIST'S JOURNEY*

Praise for Ryan Holiday

"[Ryan is a] self-help sage, who is now a sought-after guru to NFL coaches, Olympians, hip-hop stars, and Silicon Valley entrepreneurs ... [he] translates Stoicism, which had counted emperors and statesmen among its adherents during antiquity, into pithy catchphrases and digestible anecdotes for ambitious, twenty-first-century life hackers."   —ALEXANDRA ALTER, *NEW YORK TIMES*

"Holiday is an out-of-the-box thinker who likes to take chances."
—NEW YORK TIMES BOOK REVIEW

"I don't have many rules in life, but one I never break is: If Ryan Holiday writes a book, I read it as soon as I can get my hands on it."
—BRIAN KOPPELMAN, SCREENWRITER AND DIRECTOR,
ROUNDERS, OCEAN'S THIRTEEN, AND *BILLIONS*

"Ryan Holiday is one of the most promising young writers of his generation."   —GEORGE RAVELING, HALL OF FAME BASKETBALL COACH,
NIKE'S DIRECTOR OF INTERNATIONAL BASKETBALL

STILLNESS IS THE KEY

STILLNESS

IS THE KEY

RYAN HOLIDAY

PORTFOLIO/PENGUIN

Portfolio/Penguin
An imprint of Penguin Random House LLC
penguinrandomhouse.com

Most Portfolio books are available at a discount when purchased in quantity for sales
promotions or corporate use. Special editions, which include personalized covers, excerpts,
and corporate imprints, can be created when purchased in large quantities. For more
information, please call (212) 572-2232 or e-mail specialmarkets@penguinrandomhouse.com.
Your local bookstore can also assist with discounted bulk purchases using the Penguin
Random House corporate Business-to-Business program. For assistance in locating a
participating retailer, e-mail B2B@penguinrandomhouse.com.

Library of Congress Cataloging-in-Publication Data

Names: Holiday, Ryan, author.
Title: Stillness is the key / Ryan Holiday.
Description: New York : Portfolio/Penguin, [2019] | Includes bibliographical references.
Identifiers: LCCN 2019018368 (print) | LCCN 2019021767 (ebook) |
ISBN 9780525538592 (ebook) | ISBN 9780525538585 (hardcover)
Subjects: LCSH: Quietude.
Classification: LCC BJ1533.Q5 (ebook) | LCC BJ1533.Q5 H65 2019 (print) |
DDC 128/.4—dc23
LC record available at https://lccn.loc.gov/2019018368

Printed in the United States of America
13   15   17   19   20   18   16   14   12

The struggle is great, the task divine—to gain mastery, freedom, happiness, and tranquility.

—EPICTETUS

CONTENTS

PART II: SPIRIT

PART III: BODY

PREFACE

It was the late first century AD and Lucius Annaeus Seneca, Rome's most influential power broker, its greatest living playwright, and its wisest philosopher, was struggling to work.

The problem was the ear-shattering, soul-rattling noise that poured in from the street below.

Rome had always been a loud city— think New York City construction loud—but the block where Seneca was staying was a deafening cacophony of disturbances. Athletes worked out in the gymnasium underneath his suite of rooms, dropping heavy weights. A masseuse pummeled the backs of old fat men. Swimmers splashed in the water. At the entrance of the building, a pickpocket was being arrested and making a scene. Passing carriages rumbled over the stone streets, while carpenters hammered away in their shops and vendors shouted their wares. Children laughed and played. Dogs barked.

And more than the noise outside his window, there was the simple fact that Seneca's life was falling apart. It was crisis upon crisis upon crisis. Overseas unrest threatened his finances. He was getting older and could feel it. He had been pushed out of politics by his enemies, and, now on the outs with Nero, he could easily—at the emperor's whim—lose his head.

It was not, we can imagine from the perspective of our own busy lives, a great environment for a human to get anything done. Unconducive to thinking, creating, writing, or making good decisions. The noise and distractions of the empire were enough "to make me hate my very powers of hearing," Seneca told a friend.

Yet for good reason, this scene has tantalized admirers for centuries. How does a man, besieged by adversity and difficulty, not only *not* go out of his mind, but actually find the serenity to think clearly and to write incisive, perfectly crafted essays, some in that very room, which would reach millions upon millions and touch on truths that few have ever accessed?

"I have toughened my nerves against all that sort of thing," Seneca explained to that same friend about the noise. "I force my mind to concentrate, and keep it from straying to things outside itself; all outdoors may be bedlam, provided that there is no disturbance within."

Ah, isn't that what we all crave? What discipline! What focus! To be able to tune out our surroundings, to access one's full capabilities at any time, in any place, despite every difficulty? How wonderful that would be! What we'd be able to accomplish! How much happier we would be!

To Seneca and to his fellow adherents of Stoic philosophy, if a person could develop peace within themselves—if they could achieve *apatheia,* as they called it—then the whole world could be at war, and they could still think well, work well, and be well. "You may be sure that you are at peace with yourself," Seneca wrote, "when no noise reaches you, when no word shakes you out of yourself, whether it be flattery or a threat, or merely an empty sound buzzing about you with unmeaning sin." In this state, nothing could touch them (not even a deranged emperor), no emotion could disturb them, no threat could interrupt them, and every beat of the present moment would be theirs for living.

It's a powerful idea made all the more transcendent by the remarkable fact that nearly every other philosophy of the ancient world—no matter how different or distant—came to the exact same conclusion.

It wouldn't have mattered whether you were a pupil at the feet of Confucius in 500 BC, a student of the early Greek philosopher Democritus one hundred years later, or sitting in Epicurus's garden a generation after that—you would have heard equally emphatic calls for this imperturbability, unruffledness, and tranquility.

The Buddhist word for it was *upekkha.* The Muslims spoke of *aslama.* The Hebrews, *hishtavut.* The second book of the Bhagavad Gita, the epic poem of the warrior Arjuna, speaks of *samatvam,* an "evenness of mind—a peace that is ever the same." The Greeks, *euthymia* and *hesychia.* The Epicureans, *ataraxia.* The Christians, *aequanimitas.*

In English: *stillness.*

To be steady while the world spins around you. To act without frenzy. To hear only what needs to be heard. To possess quietude—exterior and interior—on command.

To tap into the *dao* and the *logos*. The Word. The Way.

Buddhism. Stoicism. Epicureanism. Christianity. Hinduism. It's all but impossible to find a philosophical school or religion that does not venerate this inner peace—this *stillness*—as the highest good and as the key to elite performance and a happy life.

And when basically *all* the wisdom of the ancient world agrees on something, only a fool would decline to listen.

STILLNESS IS THE KEY

INTRODUCTION

The call to stillness comes quietly. The modern world does not.

In addition to the clatter and chatter and intrigue and in-fighting that would be familiar to the citizens of Seneca's time, we have car horns, stereos, cell phone alarms, social media notifications, chainsaws, airplanes.

Our personal and professional problems are equally overwhelming. Competitors muscle into our industry. Our desks pile high with papers and our inboxes overflow with messages. We are always reachable, which means that arguments and updates are never far away. The news bombards us with one crisis after another on every screen we own—of which there are many. The grind of work wears us down and seems to never stop. We are overfed and undernourished. Overstimulated, overscheduled, and lonely.

Who has the power to stop? Who has time to think? Is there anyone not affected by the din and dysfunctions of our time?

While the magnitude and urgency of our struggle is modern,

it is rooted in a timeless problem. Indeed, history shows that the ability to cultivate quiet and quell the turmoil inside us, to slow the mind down, to understand our emotions, and to conquer our bodies has always been extremely difficult. "All of humanity's problems," Blaise Pascal said in 1654, "stem from man's inability to sit quietly in a room alone."

In evolution, distinct species—like birds and bats—have often evolved similar adaptations in order to survive. The same goes for the philosophical schools separated by vast oceans and distances. They developed unique paths to the same critical destination: The stillness required to become master of one's own life. To survive and thrive in any and every environment, no matter how loud or busy.

Which is why this idea of stillness is not some soft New Age nonsense or the domain of monks and sages, but in fact desperately necessary to all of us, whether we're running a hedge fund or playing in a Super Bowl, pioneering research in a new field or raising a family. It is an attainable path to enlightenment and excellence, greatness and happiness, performance as well as presence, for *every kind of person*.

Stillness is what aims the archer's arrow. It inspires new ideas. It sharpens perspective and illuminates connections. It slows the ball down so that we might hit it. It generates a vision, helps us resist the passions of the mob, makes space for gratitude and wonder. Stillness allows us to persevere. To succeed. It is the key that unlocks the insights of genius, and allows us regular folks to understand them.

The promise of this book is the location of that key . . . and a call not only for possessing stillness, but for radiating it outward like a star—like the sun—for a world that needs light more than ever.

The Key to Everything

In the early days of the American Civil War, there were a hundred competing plans for how to secure victory and whom to appoint to do it. From every general and for every battle there was an endless supply of criticism and dangerous passions—there was paranoia and fear, ego and arrogance, and very little in the way of hope.

There is a wonderful scene from those fraught first moments when Abraham Lincoln addressed a group of generals and politicians in his office at the White House. Most people at that time believed the war could only be won through enormous, decisively bloody battles in the country's biggest cities, like Richmond and New Orleans and even, potentially, Washington, D.C.

Lincoln, a man who taught himself military strategy by poring over books he checked out from the Library of Congress, laid out a map across a big table and pointed instead to Vicksburg, Mississippi, a little city deep in Southern territory. It was a fortified town high on the bluffs of the Mississippi River, held by the toughest rebel troops. Not only did it control navigation of that important waterway, but it was a juncture for a number of other important tributaries, as well as rail lines that supplied

Confederate armies and enormous slave plantations across the South.

"Vicksburg is the key," he told the crowd with the certainty of a man who had studied a matter so intensely that he could express it in the simplest of terms. "The war can never be brought to a close until that key is in our pocket."

As it happened, Lincoln turned out to be exactly right. It would take years, it would take incredible equanimity and patience, as well as ferocious commitment to his cause, but the strategy laid out in that room was what won the war and ended slavery in America forever. Every other important victory in the Civil War—from Gettysburg to Sherman's March to the Sea to Lee's surrender—was made possible because at Lincoln's instruction Ulysses S. Grant laid siege to Vicksburg in 1863, and by taking the city split the South in two and gained control of that important waterway. In his reflective, intuitive manner, without being rushed or distracted, Lincoln had seen (and held fast to) what his own advisors, and even his enemy, had missed. Because he possessed the key that unlocked victory from the rancor and folly of all those early competing plans.

In our own lives, we face a seemingly equal number of problems and are pulled in countless directions by competing priorities and beliefs. In the way of everything we hope to accomplish, personally and professionally, sit obstacles and enemies. Martin Luther King Jr. observed that there was a violent civil war raging within each and every person—between our good and bad impulses, between our ambitions and our principles, between what we can be and how hard it is to actually get there.

In those battles, in that war, stillness is the river and the railroad junction through which so much depends. *It is the key . . .*

To thinking clearly.

To seeing the whole chessboard.

To making tough decisions.

To managing our emotions.

To identifying the right goals.

To handling high-pressure situations.

To maintaining relationships.

To building good habits.

To being productive.

To physical excellence.

To feeling fulfilled.

To capturing moments of laughter and joy.

Stillness is the key to, well, just about everything.

To being a better parent, a better artist, a better investor, a better athlete, a better scientist, a better human being. To unlocking all that we are capable of in this life.

This Stillness Can Be Yours

Anyone who has concentrated so deeply that a flash of insight or inspiration suddenly visited them knows stillness. Anyone who has given their best to something, felt pride of completion, of knowing they left absolutely nothing in reserve—that's stillness. Anyone who has stepped forward with the eyes of the crowd upon them and then poured all their training into a single moment of performance—that's stillness, even if it involves active movement. Anyone who has spent time with that special, wise person, and witnessed them solve in two seconds the problem that had vexed us for months—stillness. Anyone who has walked out alone on a quiet street at night as the snow fell, and watched as the light fell softly on that snow and is warmed by the contentment of being alive—that too is stillness.

Staring at the blank page in front of us and watching as the words pour out in perfect prose, at a loss for where they came from; standing on fine white sand, looking out at the ocean, or really any part of nature, and feeling like part of something bigger than oneself; a quiet evening with a loved one; the satisfaction of having done a good turn for another person; sitting, alone with our thoughts, and seizing for the first time the ability to think about them as we were thinking them. *Stillness.*

Sure, there is a certain ineffableness to what we're talking about, to articulating the stillness that the poet Rainer Maria Rilke described as "full, complete" where "all the random and approximate were muted."

"Although we speak of attaining the *dao,*" Lao Tzu once said, "there is really nothing to obtain." Or to borrow a master's reply to a student who asked where he might find Zen: "You are seeking for an ox while you are yourself on it."

You have tasted stillness before. You have felt it in your soul. And you want more of it.

You *need* more of it.

Which is why the aim of this book is simply to show how to uncover and draw upon the stillness we already possess. It's about the cultivation of and the connection to that powerful force given to us at birth, the one that has atrophied in our modern, busy lives. This book is an attempt to answer the pressing question of our time: If the quiet moments are the best moments, and if so many wise, virtuous people have sung their praises, why are they so rare?

Well, the answer is that while we may naturally possess stillness, accessing it is not easy. One must really listen to hear it speaking to us. And answering the call requires stamina and mastery. "To hold the mind still is an enormous discipline," the late comedian Garry Shandling reminded himself in his journal as he struggled to manage fame and fortune and health problems, "one which must be faced with the greatest commitment of your life."

The pages that follow tell the stories and strategies of men and women who were just like you, who struggled as you struggle amid the noise and responsibilities of life, but managed to succeed in finding and harnessing stillness. You will hear stories of the triumphs and trials of John F. Kennedy and Fred Rogers,

Anne Frank and Queen Victoria. There will be stories about Jesus and Tiger Woods, Socrates, Napoleon, the composer John Cage, Sadaharu Oh, Rosanne Cash, Dorothy Day, Buddha, Leonardo da Vinci, and Marcus Aurelius.

We will also draw on poetry and novels, philosophical texts and scientific research. We will raid every school and every era we can to find strategies to help us direct our thoughts, process our emotions, and master our bodies. So we can do less . . . and do more. Accomplish more but need it less. Feel better and *be* better at the same time.

To achieve stillness, we'll need to focus on three domains, the timeless trinity of mind, body, soul—the head, the heart, the flesh.

In each domain, we will seek to reduce the disturbances and perturbations that make stillness impossible. To cease to be at war with the world and within ourselves, and to establish a lasting inner and outer peace instead.

You know that is what you want—and what you deserve. That's why you picked up this book.

So let us answer the call together. Let us find—let us lock into—the stillness that we seek.

PART I

MIND ◆ SPIRIT ◆ BODY

The mind is restless, Krishna, impetuous, self-willed, hard to train: to master the mind seems as difficult as to master the mighty winds.

—THE BHAGAVAD GITA

THE DOMAIN OF THE MIND

The entire world changed in the few short hours between when John F. Kennedy went to bed on October 15, 1962, and when he woke up the following morning.

Because while the president slept, the CIA identified the ongoing construction of medium- and long-range Soviet ballistic nuclear missile sites on the island of Cuba, just ninety miles from American shores. As Kennedy would tell a stunned American public days later, "Each of these missiles is capable of striking Washington, D.C., the Panama Canal, Cape Canaveral, Mexico City, or any other city in the southeastern part of the United States, in Central America, or in the Caribbean."

As Kennedy received his first briefing on what we now know as the Cuban Missile Crisis—or simply as the Thirteen Days—the president could consider only the appalling stakes. As many as seventy million people were expected to die in the first strikes between the United States and Russia. But that was just a guess—no one actually knew how terrible nuclear war would be.

What Kennedy knew for certain was that he faced an unprecedented escalation of the long-brewing Cold War between the United States and the USSR. And whatever factors had contributed to its creation, no matter how inevitable war must have appeared, it fell on him, at the very least, to just *not make things worse.* Because it might mean the end of life on planet Earth.

Kennedy was a young president born into immense privilege, raised by an aggressive father who hated to lose, in a family whose motto, they joked, was "Don't Get Mad, Get Even." With almost no executive leadership experience under his belt, it's not a surprise, then, that the first year and half of Kennedy's administration had not gone well.

In April 1961, Kennedy had tried and failed—embarrassingly so—to invade Cuba and overthrow Fidel Castro at the Bay of Pigs. Just a few months later, he was diplomatically dominated by Soviet premier Nikita Khrushchev in a series of meetings in Vienna. (Kennedy would call it the "roughest thing in my life.") Sensing his adversary's political weakness, and likely aware of the chronic physical frailty he endured from Addison's disease and back injuries suffered during World War II, Khrushchev repeatedly lied to Kennedy about any weapons being placed in Cuba, insisting that they would be for defensive purposes only.

Which is to say that during the Missile Crisis, Kennedy faced, as every leader will at some point in their tenure, a difficult test amid complicating personal and political circumstances. There were many questions: Why would Khrushchev do this? What was his endgame? What was the man possibly trying to accomplish? Was there a way to solve it? What did Kennedy's advisors think? What were Kennedy's options? Was he up to this task? Did he have what it took?

The fate of millions depended on his answers.

The advice from Kennedy's advisors was immediate and emphatic: The missile sites must be destroyed with the full might of the country's military arsenal. Every second wasted risked the safety and the reputation of the United States. After the surprise attack on the missiles, a full-scale invasion of Cuba by American troops would need to follow. This, they said, was not only more than justified by the actions of the USSR and Cuba, but it was Kennedy's *only* option.

Their logic was both primal and satisfying: Aggression must be met with aggression. Tit replied to with tat.

The only problem was that if their logic turned out to be wrong, no one would be around to account for their mistake. Because everyone would be dead.

Unlike in the early days of his presidency, when Kennedy allowed the CIA to pressure him into supporting the Bay of Pigs fiasco, this time he surprised everyone by pushing back. He had recently read Barbara Tuchman's *The Guns of August,* a book about the beginning of World War I, which imprinted on his mind the image of overconfident world leaders rushing their way into a conflict that, once started, they couldn't stop. Kennedy wanted everyone to slow down so that they could really think about the problem in front of them.

This is, in fact, the first obligation of a leader and a decision maker. Our job is not to "go with our gut" or fixate on the first impression we form about an issue. No, we need to be strong enough to resist thinking that is too neat, too plausible, and therefore almost always wrong. Because if the leader can't take the time to develop a clear sense of the bigger picture, who will? If the leader isn't thinking through all the way to the end, who is?

We can see in Kennedy's handwritten notes taken during the crisis, a sort of meditative process by which he tried to do precisely this. On numerous pages, he writes "Missile. Missile. Missile," or "Veto. Veto. Veto. Veto," or "Leaders. Leaders. Leaders." On one page, showing his desire to not act alone or selfishly: "Consensus. Consensus. Consensus. Consensus. Consensus. Consensus." On a yellow legal pad during one meeting, Kennedy drew two sailboats, calming himself with thoughts of the ocean he loved so much. Finally, on White House stationery, as if to clarify to himself the only thing that mattered, he wrote one short sentence: "We are *demanding* withdrawal of the missiles."

Perhaps it was there, as Kennedy sat with his advisors and doodled, that he remembered a passage from another book he'd read, by the strategist B. H. Liddell Hart, on nuclear strategy. In Kennedy's review of Hart's book for the *Saturday Review of Literature* a few years before, he quoted this passage:

> Keep strong, if possible. In any case, keep cool. Have unlimited patience. Never corner an opponent, and always assist him to save face. Put yourself in his shoes—so as to

see things through his eyes. Avoid self-righteousness like the devil—nothing is so self-blinding.

It became Kennedy's motto during the Missile Crisis. "I think we ought to think of why the Russians did this," he told his advisors. *What is the advantage they are trying to get?* he asked, with real interest. "Must be some major reason for the Soviets to set this up." As Arthur Schlesinger Jr., Kennedy's advisor and biographer, wrote, "With his capacity to understand the problems of others, the President could see how threatening the world might have looked to the Kremlin."

This understanding would help him respond properly to this unexpected and dangerous provocation—and give him insight into how the Soviets would react to that response.

It became clear to Kennedy that Khrushchev put the missiles in Cuba because he believed Kennedy was weak. But that didn't mean the Russians believed their own position was particularly strong. Only a desperate nation would take such a risk, Kennedy realized. Armed with this insight, which came through long discussions with his team—designated as ExComm—he began to formulate an action plan.

Clearly, a military strike was the most irrevocable of all the options (nor, according to his advisors, was it likely to be 100 percent effective). What would happen after that, Kennedy wondered? How many soldiers would die in an invasion? How would the world respond to a larger country invading a smaller one, even if it was to deter a nuclear threat? What would the Russians do to save face or protect their soldiers on the island?

These questions pointed Kennedy toward a blockade of Cuba. Nearly half of his advisors opposed this less aggressive move, but he favored it precisely because it preserved his options.

The blockade also embodied the wisdom of one of Kennedy's favorite expressions: It *used time as a tool*. It gave both sides a chance to examine the stakes of the crisis and offered Khrushchev the opportunity to reevaluate his impression of Kennedy's supposed weakness.

Some would later attack Kennedy for this choice, too. Why challenge Russia at all? Why were the missiles such a big deal? Didn't the United States have plenty of their own pointed at the Soviets? Kennedy was not unsympathetic to this argument, but as he explained to the American public in an address on October 22, it wasn't possible to simply back down:

> The 1930s taught us a clear lesson: Aggressive conduct, if allowed to go unchecked and unchallenged, ultimately leads to war. This nation is opposed to war. We are also true to our word. Our unswerving objective, therefore, must be to prevent the use of these missiles against this or any other country, and to secure their withdrawal or elimination from the Western Hemisphere. . . . We will not prematurely or unnecessarily risk the costs of world-wide nuclear war in which even the fruits of victory

would be ashes in our mouth—but neither will we shrink
from that risk at any time it must be faced.

What's most remarkable about this conclusion is how calmly
Kennedy came to it. Despite the enormous stress of the situation, we can hear in tapes and see in transcripts and photos
taken at the time just how collaborative and open everyone was.
No fighting, no raised voices. No finger-pointing (and when
things did get tense, Kennedy laughed it off). Kennedy didn't let
his own ego dominate the discussions, nor did he allow anyone
else's to. When he sensed that his presence was stifling his advisors' ability to speak honestly, he left the room so they could de-
bate and brainstorm freely. Reaching across party lines and past
rivalries, he consulted openly with the three still-living ex-
presidents and invited the previous secretary of state, Dean
Acheson, into the top-secret meetings as an equal.

In the tensest moments, Kennedy sought solitude in the
White House Rose Garden (afterward, he would thank the gar-
dener for her important contributions during the crisis). He
would go for long swims, both to clear his mind and to think. He
sat in his specially made rocking chair in the Oval Office, bathed
in the light of those enormous windows, easing the pain in his
back so that it might not add to the fog of (cold) war that had
descended so thickly over Washington and Moscow.

There is a picture of Kennedy with his back to the room,
hunched over, leaning both fists on the big desk he had been

chosen by millions of voters to occupy. This is a man with the fate of the world on his shoulders. He has been provoked by a nuclear superpower in a surprise act of bad faith. Critics are questioning his courage. There are political considerations, personal considerations, there are more factors than any one person should be able to weigh at one time.

Yet he lets none of this rush him. None of it will cloud his judgment or deter him from doing the right thing. He is the stillest guy in the room.

Kennedy would need to stay that way, because simply *deciding* on the blockade was only the first step. Next came announcing and enforcing this five-hundred-mile no-go zone around Cuba (which he brilliantly called a "quarantine" to underplay the more aggressive implications of a "blockade"). There would be more belligerent accusations from the Russians and confrontations at the UN. Congressional leaders voiced their doubts. One hundred thousand troops still had to be readied in Florida as a contingency.

Then there would be the actual provocations. A Russian tanker ship approached the quarantine line. Russian submarines surfaced. An American U-2 spy plane was shot down over Cuba, and the pilot killed.

The two biggest and most powerful countries in the world were "eyeball to eyeball." It was actually scarier and more dire than anyone knew—some of the Soviet missiles, which had been previously thought to be only partly assembled, were armed and ready. Even if this wasn't known, the awful danger could be *felt*.

Would Kennedy's emotions get the best of him? Would he blink? Would he break?

No. He wouldn't.

"It isn't the first step that concerns me," he said to his advisors as much as to himself, "but both sides escalating to the fourth and fifth step—and we don't go to the sixth because there is no one around to do so. We must remind ourselves we are embarking on a very hazardous course."

The space Kennedy gave Khrushchev to breathe and think paid off just in time. On October 26, eleven days into the crisis, the Soviet premier wrote Kennedy a letter saying that he now saw that the two of them were pulling on a rope with a knot in the middle—a knot of war. The harder each pulled, the less likely it would be that they could ever untie it, and eventually there would be no choice but to cut the rope with a sword. And then Khrushchev provided an even more vivid analogy, one as true in geopolitics as it is in everyday life: "If people do not display statesmanlike wisdom," he said, "they will eventually reach the point where they will clash, like blind moles, and then mutual annihilation will commence."

Suddenly, the crisis was over as quickly as it began. The Russians, realizing that their position was untenable and that their test of U.S. resolve had failed, made signs that they would negotiate—that they would remove the missiles. The ships stopped dead in the water. Kennedy was ready too. He pledged that the United States would not invade Cuba, giving the Russians and their allies a win. In secret, he also let the Russians know that he was willing to remove American missiles in Turkey, but would do so in several months' time so as not to give the impression that he could be pressured into abandoning an ally.

With clear thinking, wisdom, patience, and a keen eye for the root of a complex, provocative conflict, Kennedy had saved the world from a nuclear holocaust.

We might say that Kennedy, if only for this brief period of a little less than two weeks, managed to achieve that stage of clarity spoken about in the ancient Chinese text *The Daodejing*. As he stared down nuclear annihilation, he was:

> *Careful as someone crossing an iced-over stream.*
> *Alert as a warrior in enemy territory.*
> *Courteous as a guest.*
> *Fluid as melting ice.*
> *Shapable as a block of wood.*
> *Receptive as a valley.*
> *Clear as a glass of water.*

The Daoists would say that he had stilled the muddied water in his mind until he could see through it. Or to borrow the image from the emperor Marcus Aurelius, the Stoic philosopher who himself had stared down countless crises and challenges, Kennedy had been "like the rock that the waves keep crashing over. It stands, unmoved and the raging of the sea falls still around it."

Each of us will, in our own lives, face crisis. The stakes may be lower, but to us they will matter. A business on the brink of collapse. An acrimonious divorce. A decision about the future of our career. A moment where the whole game depends on us. These situations will call upon all our mental resources. An emotional, reactive response—an unthinking, half-baked response—will not cut it. Not if we want to get it right. Not if we want to perform at our best.

What we will need then is that same stillness that Kennedy drew upon. His calmness. His open-mindedness. His empathy. His clarity about what really mattered.

In these situations we must:

- Be fully present.
- Empty our mind of preconceptions.
- Take our time.
- Sit quietly and reflect.
- Reject distraction.
- Weigh advice against the counsel of our convictions.
- Deliberate without being paralyzed.

We must cultivate mental stillness to succeed in life and to successfully navigate the many crises it throws our way.

It will not be easy. But it is essential.

For the rest of his short life, Kennedy worried that people would learn the wrong lessons from his actions during the Missile Crisis. It wasn't that he had stood up to the Soviets and threatened them with superior weapons until they backed down. Instead, calm and rational leadership had prevailed over rasher, reckless voices. The crisis was resolved thanks to a mastery of his own thinking, and the thinking of those underneath him—and it was these traits that America would need to call on repeatedly in the years to come. The lesson was one not of *force* but of the power of patience, alternating confidence and humility, foresight and presence, empathy and unbending conviction, restraint and toughness, and quiet solitude combined with wise counsel.

How much better would the world be with more of this behavior? How much better would your own life be?

Kennedy, like Lincoln, was not born with this stillness. He was a defiant troublemaker in high school, a dilettante for most of college and even as a senator. He had his demons and he made plenty of mistakes. But with hard work—work you are capable of doing too—he overcame those shortcomings and developed the equanimity that served him so well over those terrifying thirteen days. It was work in just a few categories that nearly everyone else neglects.

Which is where we will now turn our focus—toward mastering what we will call in this section "the domain of the mind"—because everything we do depends on getting that right.

BECOME PRESENT

Trust no future, howe'er pleasant!
Let the dead Past bury its dead!
Act,—act in the living present!
Heart within, and God o'erhead!

—HENRY WADSWORTH LONGFELLOW

The decision in 2010 to title Marina Abramović's four-decade retrospective at MoMA in New York City *The Artist Is Present* all but preordained the monumental performance that would come out of it. Naturally, Marina would have to be present in one way or another.

But no one would have dared think that she would literally be there . . . for all of it.

Who could conceive that a human could sit silently in a chair, completely still, for a total of 750 hours over 79 days directly across from 1,545 strangers, without aid, without distraction, without so much as a way to go to the bathroom? That she would want to do this? That she would pull it off?

As her former lover and collaborator Ulay said when he was asked what he thought of the possibility, "I have no thoughts. Only respect."

The performance was as simple as it was straightforward. Marina, aged sixty-three, her long hair braided and over her shoulder, walked into the cavernous room, sat down in a hard wooden chair, and simply stared at the person across from her. One after another they came, hour after hour, day in and day out, for nearly three months. Each time, she looked down, gathered herself, and then looked up afresh at the new face.

As Marina would say of her art, "The proposition here is just to empty the self. To be able to be present."

Is it really that hard—to be present? What's so special about that?

No one who was in the audience, who sat across from her, would ask such questions. For those souls lucky enough to see the performance in person, it was a near religious experience. To experience another person fully in the moment is a rare thing. To feel them engage with you, to be giving all their energy to you, as though there is nothing else that matters in the world, is rarer still. To see them do it for so long, so intensely?

Many viewers cried. Each one said the hours in line were worth it. It was like looking in a kind of mirror, where they could feel their own life for the first time.

Imagine: If Marina's mind drifted, if she daydreamed, the

person across from her could immediately sense that she was somewhere else. If she slowed her mind and body down too much, she might have fallen asleep. If she allowed for normal bodily sensations—hunger, discomfort, pain, the urge to go to the bathroom—it would be impossible not to move or get up. If she began to think of how much time was left in the day's performance, time would slow to an intolerable crawl. So with monklike discipline and warriorlike strength she ignored these distractions to exist exclusively in the present moment. She had to be where her feet were; she had to care about the person across from her and the experience they were sharing more than anything else in the world.

"People don't understand that the hardest thing is actually doing something that is close to nothing," Abramović said about the performance. "It demands all of you . . . there is no object to hide behind. It's just you."

Being present demands all of us. It's not nothing. It may be the hardest thing in the world.

As we stand on the podium, about to give a speech, our mind is focused not on our task but on what everyone will think of us. How does that not affect our performance? As we struggle with a crisis, our mind repeats on a loop just how unfair this is, how insane it is that it keeps happening and how it can't go on. Why are we draining ourselves of essential emotional and mental energies right when we need them most?

Even during a quiet evening at home, all we're thinking about is the list of improvements that need to be made. There may be a beautiful sunset, but instead of taking it in, we're *taking a picture of it.*

We are not present . . . and so we miss out. On life. On being our best. On *seeing* what's there.

Many of the people in line to see Marina Abramović's performance accidentally illustrate this phenomenon. Rushing in as the doors opened, they zoomed past equally impressive pieces from her career so that they could be first for the "special" one. In line, they fidgeted endlessly and chatted with each other, trying to kill time as the hours ticked by. They napped, leaning up against one another. They checked their phones . . . and then checked them again. They planned what they would do when it was their turn and speculated about what it would be like. Some of them worked in secret on little stunts they hoped would bring them fifteen seconds of fame.

How much ordinary wonderfulness they closed their minds to.

It makes you wonder: After they had their transcendent experience with Marina—coming face-to-face with real presence—when they left the museum and walked out into the busy New York City street, did they breathe in anew the vibrant rhythm of the urban jungle, or, more likely, did they immediately resume their busy lives, full of distractions, anxiety, dreams, insecurities, and ego?

In short, did they do exactly what all of us do most of every single day?

We do not live in *this* moment. We, in fact, try desperately to get out of it—by thinking, doing, talking, worrying, remembering, hoping, whatever. We pay thousands of dollars to have a device in our pocket to ensure that we are never bored. We sign up for endless activities and obligations, chase money and accomplishments, all with the naïve belief that at the end of it will be happiness.

Tolstoy observed that love can't exist off in the future. Love is only real if it's happening right now. If you think about it, that's true for basically everything we think, feel, or do. The best athletes, in the biggest games, are completely *there*. They are within themselves, within the now.

Remember, there's no greatness in the future. Or clarity. Or insight. Or happiness. Or peace. There is only this moment.

Not that we mean literally sixty seconds. The real present moment is what we choose to exist in, instead of lingering on the past or fretting about the future. It's however long we can push away the impressions of what's happened before and what we worry or hope might occur at some other time. Right now can be a few minutes or a morning or a year—if you can stay in it that long.

As Laura Ingalls Wilder said, *now is now*. It can never be anything else.

Seize it!

Who is so talented that they can afford to bring only part of themselves to bear on a problem or opportunity? Whose relationships are so strong that they can get away with not showing up? Who is so certain that they'll get another moment that they can confidently skip over this one? The less energy we waste regretting the past or worrying about the future, the more energy we will have for what's in front of us.

We want to learn to see the world like an artist: While other people are oblivious to what surrounds them, the artist really *sees*. Their mind, fully engaged, notices the way a bird flies or the way a stranger holds their fork or a mother looks at her child. They have no thoughts of the morrow. All they are thinking about is how to capture and communicate this experience.

An artist is *present*. And from this stillness comes brilliance.

This moment we are experiencing right now is a gift (that's why we call it *the present*). Even if it is a stressful, trying experience—it could be our last. So let's develop the ability to be in it, to put everything we have into appreciating the plentitude of the now.

Don't reject a difficult or boring moment because it is not exactly what you want. Don't waste a beautiful moment because you are insecure or shy. Make what you can of what you have been given. Live what can be lived. That's what excellence is. That's what presence makes possible.

In meditation, teachers instruct students to focus on their breath. *In and out. In and out.* In sports, coaches speak about "the process"—this play, this drill, this rep. Not just because this moment is special, but because you can't do your best if your mind is elsewhere.

We would do well to follow this in our own lives. Jesus told his disciples not to worry about tomorrow, because tomorrow will take care of itself. Another way of saying that is: You have plenty on your plate right now. Focus on that, no matter how small or insignificant it is. Do the very best you can right now. Don't think about what detractors may say. Don't dwell or needlessly complicate. Be here. Be *all* of you.

Be present.

And if you've had trouble with this in the past? That's okay.

That's the nice thing about the present. It keeps showing up to give you a second chance.

LIMIT YOUR INPUTS

A wealth of information creates a poverty of attention.

—HERBERT SIMON

As a general, Napoleon made it his habit to delay responding to the mail. His secretary was instructed to wait three weeks before opening any correspondence. When he finally did hear what was in a letter, Napoleon loved to note how many supposedly "important" issues had simply resolved themselves and no longer required a reply.

While Napoleon was certainly an eccentric leader, he was never negligent in his duties or out of touch with his government or his soldiers. But in order to be active and aware of what actually mattered, he had to be selective about who and what kind of information got access to his brain.

In a similar vein, he told messengers never to wake him with *good news*. Bad news, on the other hand—that is to say, an unfolding crisis or an urgent development that negatively impacted his campaign—was to be brought to him immediately. "Rouse me instantly," he said, "for then there is not a moment to be lost."

These were both brilliant accommodations to the reality of life for a busy person: There is way too much coming at us. In order to think clearly, it is essential that each of us figures out how to filter out the inconsequential from the essential. It's not enough to be inclined toward deep thought and sober analysis; a leader must create time and space for it.

In the modern world, this is not easy. In the 1990s, political scientists began to study what they called the "CNN Effect." Breathless, twenty-four-hour media coverage makes it considerably harder for politicians and CEOs to be anything but reactive. There's too much information, every trivial detail is magnified under the microscope, speculation is rampant—and the mind is overwhelmed.

The CNN Effect is now a problem for everyone, not just presidents and generals. Each of us has access to more information than we could ever reasonably use. We tell ourselves that it's part of our job, that we have to be "on top of things," and so we give up precious time to news, reports, meetings, and other forms of feedback. Even if we're not glued to a television, we're still surrounded by gossip and drama and other distractions.

We must stop this.

"If you wish to improve," Epictetus once said, "be content to appear clueless or stupid in extraneous matters."

Napoleon was content with being behind on his mail, even if

it upset some people or if he missed out on some gossip, because it meant that trivial problems had to resolve themselves without him. We need to cultivate a similar attitude—give things a little space, don't consume news in real time, be a season or two behind on the latest trend or cultural phenomenon, don't let your inbox lord over your life.

The important stuff will still be important by the time you get to it. The unimportant will have made its insignificance obvious (or simply disappeared). Then, with stillness rather than needless urgency or exhaustion, you will be able to sit down and give what deserves consideration your *full* attention.

There is ego in trying to stay up on everything, whether it's an acclaimed television show, the newest industry rumor, the smartest hot take, or the hottest crisis in [the Middle East, Africa, Asia, the climate, the World Bank, the NATO Summit, ad infinitum]. There is ego in trying to appear the most informed person in the room, the one with all the gossip, who knows every single thing that's happening in everyone's life.

Not only does this cost us our peace of mind, but there's a serious opportunity cost too. If we were stiller, more confident, had the longer view, what truly meaningful subject could we dedicate our mental energy to?

In her diary in 1942, Dorothy Day, the Catholic nun and social activist, admonished herself much the same. "Turn off your radio," she wrote, "put away your daily paper. Read one review of events and spend time reading." *Books,* spend time reading books—that's what she meant. Books full of wisdom.

Though this too can be overdone.

The verse from John Ferriar:

> *What wild desires, what restless torments seize*
> *The hapless man, who feels the book-disease.*

The point is, it's very difficult to think or act clearly (to say nothing of being happy) when we are drowning in information. It's why lawyers attempt to bury the other side in paper. It's why intelligence operatives flood the enemy with propaganda, so they'll lose the scent of the truth. It's not a coincidence that the goal of these tactics is casually referred to as analysis *paralysis*.

Yet we do this to ourselves!

A century and a half after Napoleon, another great general and, later, head of state, Dwight D. Eisenhower, struggled to manage the torrent of facts and fiction that was thrown at him. His solution was strict adherence to the chain of command when it came to information. No one was to hand him unopened mail, no one was to just throw half-explored problems at him. Too much depended on the stillness within that he needed to operate to allow such haphazard information flow. One of his innovations was to organize information and problems into what's now called the "Eisenhower Box," a matrix that orders our priorities by their ratio of urgency and importance.

Much that was happening in the world or on the job, Eisenhower found, was urgent but not important. Meanwhile, most of what was truly important was not remotely time-sensitive.

Categorizing his inputs helped him organize his staff around what was important versus what *seemed* urgent, allowed them to be strategic rather than reactive, a mile deep on what mattered rather than an inch on too many things.

Indeed, the first thing great chiefs of staff do—whether it's for a general or a president or the CEO of a local bank—is limit the amount of people who have access to the boss. They become gatekeepers: no more drop-ins, tidbits, and stray reports. So the boss can see the big picture. So the boss has time and room to think.

Because if the boss doesn't? Well, then nobody can.

In his *Meditations,* Marcus Aurelius says, "Ask yourself at every moment, 'Is this necessary?'"

Knowing what not to think about. What to ignore and not to do. It's your first and most important job.

Thich Nhat Hanh:

> Before we can make deep changes in our lives, we have to look into our diet, our way of consuming. We have to live in such a way that we stop consuming the things that poison us and intoxicate us. Then we will have the strength to allow the best in us to arise, and we will no longer be victims of anger, of frustration.

It's as true of food as it is of information.

There's a great saying: *Garbage in, garbage out.* If you want good output, you have to watch over the inputs.

This will take discipline. It will not be easy.

This means fewer alerts and notifications. It means blocking incoming texts with the Do Not Disturb function and funneling emails to subfolders. It means questioning that "open door" policy, or even *where you live*. It means pushing away selfish people who bring needless drama into our lives. It means studying the world more *philosophically*—that is, with a long-term perspective—rather than following events second by second.

The way you feel when you awake early in the morning and your mind is fresh and as yet unsoiled by the noise of the outside world—that's space worth protecting. So too is the zone you lock into when you're really working well. Don't let intrusions bounce you out of it. Put up barriers. Put up the proper chuting to direct what's urgent and unimportant to the right people.

Walker Percy, one of the last great southern novelists, has a powerful passage in *Lancelot,* based on Percy's own struggle with idleness and addiction to entertainment. In the book, the harried narrator walks outside of his Mississippi mansion and, for the first time in years, simply stops. He steps outside his bubble and experiences the moment. "Can a man stand alone, naked, and at his ease, wrist flexed at his side like Michelangelo's David, without assistance, without diversion . . . in silence?" he asks.

> Yes. It was possible to stand. Nothing happened. I listened. There was no sound: no boats on the river, no trucks on the road, not even cicadas. What if I didn't listen to the

news? I didn't. Nothing happened. I realized I had been afraid of the silence.

It is in this stillness that we can be present and finally see truth. It is in this stillness that we can hear the voice inside us.

How different would the world look if people spent as much time listening to their conscience as they did to chattering broadcasts? If they could respond to the calls of their convictions as quickly as we answer the dings and rings of technology in our pockets?

All this noise. All this information. All these inputs.

We are afraid of the silence. We are afraid of looking stupid. We are afraid of missing out. We are afraid of being the bad guy who says, "Nope, not interested."

We'd rather make ourselves miserable than make ourselves a priority, than be our best selves.

Than be still . . . and in charge of our own information diet.

EMPTY THE MIND

> To become empty is to become one with the divine—
> this is the Way.
>
> —AWA KENZO

Shawn Green began his third season with the Los Angeles Dodgers in 2002 in the worst slump of his Major League Baseball career. The media was out for blood, and so were the fans, who booed him at the plate. Dodgers management began to doubt him too. The man was making $14 million a year and he could not hit.

After *weeks* of intense hitting famine, would he be benched? Traded? Sent down to the minors?

All this was racing through Green's mind, as it would race through the mind of anyone struggling at work. That little voice: *What's wrong with you? Why can't you get this right? Did you lose your touch?*

Hitting a baseball is already a nearly inconceivable feat. It requires the batter to see, process, decide, swing at, and connect with a tiny ball traveling at speeds north of 90 miles per hour from an elevated position sixty feet away. *Four hundred milliseconds*. That's how long it takes for the ball to travel from the mound to the batter. To be able to swing and hit it literally defies physics—it's the single hardest act in all of sports.

The anxiety and doubts in a slump make it even harder. Yogi Berra's warning: "It's impossible to hit and think at the same time."

For Green, the ball began to look smaller and smaller the longer he went without a hit. But it was Buddhism, which he had long practiced, that Shawn leaned on to prevent this vicious cycle from destroying his career. Instead of giving in to those churning thoughts—instead of trying harder and harder—he tried to clear his mind entirely. Instead of fighting the slump, he was going to try not to think about it at all.

It seems crazy, but it isn't. "Man is a thinking reed," D. T. Suzuki, one of the early popularizers of Buddhism in the West, once said, "but his great works are done when he is not calculating and thinking. 'Childlikeness' has to be restored with long years of training in the art of self-forgetfulness. When this is attained, man thinks yet he does not think."

The way out of the slump wasn't to consult experts or redesign his swing. Shawn Green knew he had to get rid of the toxic thinking that had knocked him off his game in the first place—the thinking about his big contract, the expectations for how he wanted the season to go, the stress at home, or the critics in the media.

He had to push all that out of his mind. He had to let his training take over.

On May 23, 2002, Green was struggling to do exactly that. It was the rubber match in a series against the Brewers. The Dodgers had eked out a 1–0 victory the night before, and lost the night before that. Green's own hitting was sporadic and discouraging. So when he got to the ballpark that morning, he worked to give himself a fresh start. First in the batting cage, and then at the batting tee, he slowly, patiently, quietly cleared his mind. With each swing, he tried to focus on the mechanics, the placement of his feet, really planting himself where his feet were—not thinking of the past, not worrying about what was coming in the future, not thinking about the fans or how he wanted to hit the ball. Really, he wasn't thinking at all. Instead, he repeated an old Zen proverb to himself: *Chop wood, carry water. Chop wood, carry water. Chop wood, carry water.*

Don't overanalyze. Do the work.

Don't think. *Hit.*

In his first at bat on that day, Green took two strikes in the first two pitches. His mind burbled a bit—*Is the slump going to keep going, is this ever going to end, why can't I get this right?*—but he let those wild horses run right on by, waiting for the dust they kicked up to settle. He breathed in, emptied his mind again—as empty as the seats in the stadium during his pregame ritual.

Then he got back to work. On the third pitch—*CRACK!* A solid double down the right-field line.

In the second inning, Green got an inside fastball. He planted his front foot and focused only on that, on the feeling of being nailed to the ground. He watched the pitch, and swung. The ball was soon going back out the other direction, high up over the right-field wall. Three runs came in along with it. In the fourth inning, he hit another homer up in the walkway over right-center field. In the fifth inning, he hit a home run deep into left field. Opposite field, a sign that a hitter is really starting to dial in. In the eighth inning, he hit a long single.

The slump was no more.

Five for five in his at bats, and the manager wanted to send him home for the day. Green asked for another at bat.

Now his mind was tempted to race in a different direction, his brain filled with congratulations instead of doubts. *You're killing it. How exciting is this? Are you going to get another hit? You could set a record!*

Just like the overactive voice in a slump, the voice in a streak is an equally deleterious racing mental loop. Both get in the way. Both make a hard thing harder.

As Shawn Green stepped into the batter's box for the sixth and final time, he said to himself, "There's no sense in thinking now." He cleared his mind, and enjoyed himself like a kid at a Little League game.

No pressure. Just presence. Just happy to be there.

On the third pitch, he got a dipping cutter that sank low and inside, below knee level. For lefties, like Green, when they are in a slump, that area of the hitting zone is like a black hole. When they're locked in, it's the wheelhouse. Green connected, with a swing that even one of the coaches said looked like it was happening in slow motion. Every part of the batter was behind the bat, mentally and physically—and the ball was launched deep, deep into right-center field. He hit it a mile. It slammed high off the back wall of the enclosed stadium and bounced back onto the field.

As Green's teammates went nuts in the dugout, he kept his head down and rounded the bases with the same calm, deliberate trot as in his previous three home runs. You couldn't tell from the lack of celebrating, but he was in that moment only the fourteenth player in history ever to hit four home runs in a single game. Six for six, with nineteen total bases and seven runs batted in, perhaps the single greatest one-game performance in baseball. The entire crowd of 26,728 people—at an away game—rose for a standing ovation. But Green was already clearing that all away, and coming back to his routine. He took off his batting gloves and swept the experience from his mind, keeping it empty to use in the next game.*

Shawn Green is hardly the first Buddhist baseball player. Sadaharu Oh, the greatest home run hitter in the history of

---

*In his next two games, Green would hit three more home runs. He was 11 for 13 in three games with seven home runs. On the last home run he broke his bat, which now sits in the Baseball Hall of Fame.

baseball, was one too. The goal of Zen, his master taught him, was to "achieve a void . . . noiseless, colorless, heatless void"—to get to that state of emptiness, whether it was on the mound or in the batter's box or at practice.

Before that, Zhuang Zhou, the Chinese philosopher, said, "Tao is in the emptiness. Emptiness is the fast of the mind." Marcus Aurelius once wrote about "cutting free of impressions that cling to the mind, free of the future and the past," to become the "sphere rejoicing in its perfect stillness." But if you saw those words in the first paragraph of the write-up for the Dodgers-Brewers game in the *Los Angeles Times* the next day, they would have made perfect sense. Epictetus, Marcus's philosophical predecessor, was in fact speaking about sports when he said, "If we're anxious or nervous when we make the catch or throw, what will become of the game, and how can one maintain one's composure; how can one see what is coming next?"

As is true in athletics, so too in life.

Yes, thinking is essential. Expert knowledge is undoubtedly key to the success of any leader or athlete or artist. The problem is that, unthinkingly, we think too much. The "wild and whirling words" of our subconscious get going and suddenly there's no room for our training (or anything else). We're overloaded, overwhelmed, and distracted . . . by our own mind!

But if we can clear space, if we can consciously empty our mind, as Green did, insights and breakthroughs happen. The perfect swing connects perfectly with the ball.

There is a beautiful paradox to this idea of *void*.

The Daodejing points out that when clay is formed around emptiness, it becomes a pitcher that can hold water. Water from the pitcher is poured into a cup, which is itself formed around emptiness. The room this all happens in is itself four walls formed around emptiness.

Do you see? By relying on what's not there, we actually have something worth using. During the recording of her album *Interiors,* the musician Rosanne Cash posted a simple sign over the doorway of the studio. "Abandon Thought, All Ye Who Enter Here." Not because she wanted a bunch of unthinking idiots working with her, but because she wanted everyone involved—included herself—to go deeper than whatever was on the surface of their minds. She wanted them to be present, connected to the music, and not lost in their heads.

Imagine if Kennedy had spent the Cuban Missile Crisis obsessing over the Bay of Pigs. Imagine if Shawn Green had tried frantically to re-create his swing because it wasn't working, or if he had faced those pitchers with a racing mind, filled with insecurities and desperation. We've all experienced that—*Don't mess up. Don't mess up. Don't forget,* we say to ourselves—and what happens? We do exactly what we were trying *not* to do!

Whatever you face, whatever you're doing will require, first and foremost, that you don't defeat yourself. That you don't make it harder by overthinking, by needless doubts, or by second-guessing.

That space between your ears—that's yours. You don't just have to control what gets in, you also have to control what goes on *in* there. You have to protect it from yourself, from your own thoughts. Not with sheer force, but rather with a kind of gentle, persistent sweeping. Be the librarian who says "Shhh!" to the rowdy kids, or tells the jerk on his phone to please take it outside.

Because the mind is an important and sacred place.

Keep it clean and clear.

SLOW DOWN, THINK DEEPLY

> With my sighted eye I see what's before me, and with
> my unsighted eye I see what's hidden.
>
> —ALICE WALKER

In the intro sequence of the beloved children's show *Mister Rogers' Neighborhood*, the first interior shot does not show the host. Instead, in the beat before Fred Rogers appears on the screen singing his cheerful song about being a good neighbor, viewers see a traffic light, blinking yellow.

For more than thirty years and for nearly a thousand episodes, this subtle piece of symbolism opened the show. If as a hint, it went over the heads of most people watching, viewers were still primed to get the message. Because whether Fred Rogers was speaking on camera, playing in the Neighborhood of Make-Believe with King Friday the Puppet, or singing one of his trademark songs, just about every frame of the show seemed to say: *Slow down. Be considerate. Be aware.*

As a child at Latrobe Elementary School in Pennsylvania, Fred Rogers had been a victim of vicious bullying. Kids picked on him because of his weight and because he was sensitive about it. It was a horrible experience, but this pain spurred his groundbreaking work in public television. "I began a lifelong search for what is essential," he said about his childhood, "what it is about my neighbor that doesn't meet the eye." He even framed a print of that idea on the wall of his production studio in Pittsburgh, a snippet from one of his favorite quotes: *L'essentiel est invisible pour les yeux.*

What's essential is invisible to the eye.

That is: Appearances are misleading. First impressions are too. We are disturbed and deceived by what's on the surface, by what others see. Then we make bad decisions, miss opportunities, or feel scared or upset. Particularly when we don't slow down and take the time to really look.

Think about Khrushchev on the other side of the Cuban Missile Crisis. What provoked his incredible overreach? A poor reading of his opponent's mettle. A rush to action. Shoddy thinking about how his own actions would be interpreted on the world stage. It was a nearly fatal miscalculation, as most rush jobs are.

Epictetus talked about how the job of a philosopher is to take our impressions—what we see, hear, and think—and put them to the test. He said we needed to hold up our thoughts and examine them, to make sure we weren't being led astray by appearances or missing what couldn't be seen by the naked eye.

Indeed, it is in Stoicism and Buddhism and countless other schools that we find the same analogy: The world is like muddy water. To see through it, we have to let things settle. We can't be disturbed by initial appearances, and if we are patient and still, the truth will be revealed to us.

That's what Mr. Rogers taught children to do—starting a crucial habit as early as possible in their lives. In countless episodes, Rogers would take a topic—whether it was self-worth or how crayons were made, divorce or having fun—and walk his young viewers through what was really happening and what it meant. He seemed to naturally know how a kid's mind would process information, and he'd help them clear up understandable confusion or fears. He taught empathy and critical reasoning skills. He reassured his viewers that they could figure just about anything out if they took the time to work through it—with him, together.

It's a message he shared with adults too. "Just think," Rogers once wrote to a struggling friend. "Just be quiet and think. It'll make all the difference in the world."

There is, on the surface, a contradiction here. On the one hand, the Buddhists say we must empty our minds to be fully present. We'll never get anything done if we are paralyzed by overthinking. On the other hand, we must look and think and study deeply if we are ever to truly *know* (and if we are to avoid falling into the destructive patterns that harm so many people).

In fact, this is not a contradiction at all. It's just life.

We have to get better at thinking, deliberately and intentionally, about the big questions. On the complicated things. On understanding what's really going on with a person, or a situation, or with life itself.

We have to do the kind of thinking that 99 percent of the population is just not doing, and we have to stop doing the destructive thinking that they spend 99 percent of their time doing.

The eighteenth-century Zen master Hakuin was highly critical of teachers who believed that enlightenment was simply a matter of thinking *nothing*. Instead, he wanted his students to think really, really hard. This is why he assigned them perplexing *kōans* like "What is the sound of one hand clapping?" and "What did your face look like before you were born?" and "Does the dog have the Buddha nature?"

These questions defy easy answers, and that's the point. By taking the time to meditate on them deeply, in some cases for days and weeks or even years, students put their mind in such a clarified state that deeper truths emerge, and enlightenment commences (and even if they don't get all the way there, they are stronger for having tried).

"Suddenly," Hakuin promised his students, "unexpectedly your teeth sink in. Your body will pour with cold sweat. At the instant, it will all become clear." The word for this was *satori*—an illuminating insight when the inscrutable is revealed, when an essential truth becomes obvious and inescapable.

Couldn't we all use a bit more of that?

Well, no one gets to *satori* going a million miles a minute. No one gets there by focusing on what's obvious, or by sticking with the first thought that pops into their head. To see what matters, you really have to look. To understand it, you have to really think. It takes real work to grasp what is invisible to just about everyone else.

This will not only be advantageous to your career and your business, but it will also help you find peace and comfort.

There is another great insight from Fred Rogers, which now goes viral each time there is another unspeakable tragedy. "Always look for the helpers," he explained to his viewers who were scared or disillusioned by the news. "There's always someone who is trying to help. . . . The world is full of doctors and nurses, police and firemen, volunteers, neighbors and friends who are ready to jump in to help when things go wrong."

Make no mistake—this was not some glib reassurance. Rogers, building on advice from his own mother when he was a child, had managed to find comfort and goodness inside an event that would provoke only pain and anger and fear in other people. And he figured out how to communicate it in a way that continues to make the world a better place long after his death.

So much of the distress we feel comes from reacting instinctually instead of acting with conscientious deliberation. So much of what we get wrong comes from the same place. We're reacting to shadows. We're taking as certainties impressions we have yet to test. We're not stopping to put on our glasses and really *look*.

Your job, after you have emptied your mind, is to slow down and think. To really think, on a regular basis.

... Think about what's important to you.

... Think about what's actually going on.

... Think about what might be hidden from view.

... Think about what the rest of the chessboard looks like.

... Think about what the meaning of life really is.

The choreographer Twyla Tharp provides an exercise for us to follow:

> Sit alone in a room and let your thoughts go wherever they will. Do this for one minute.... Work up to ten minutes a day of this mindless mental wandering. Then start paying attention to your thoughts to see if a word or goal materializes. If it doesn't, extend the exercise to eleven minutes, then twelve, then thirteen ... until you find the length of time you need to ensure that something interesting will come to mind. The Gaelic phrase for this state of mind is "quietness without loneliness."

If you invest the time and mental energy, you'll not only find what's interesting (or your next creative project), you'll find truth. You'll find what other people have missed. You'll find solutions to the problems we face—whether it's insight to the logic of the Soviets and their missiles in Cuba, or how to move your business forward, or how to make sense of senseless violence.

These are answers that must be fished from the depths. And what is fishing but slowing down? Being both relaxed and highly attuned to your environment? And ultimately, catching hold of what lurks below the surface and reeling it in?

START JOURNALING

Keep a notebook. Travel with it, eat with it, sleep with
it. Slap into it every stray thought that flutters up into
your brain.

—JACK LONDON

or her thirteenth birthday, a precocious German refugee
named Anne Frank was given a small red-and-white "auto-
graph book" by her parents. Although the pages were designed
to collect the signatures and memories of friends, she knew
from the moment she first saw it in a store window that she
would use it as a journal. As Anne wrote in her first entry on
June 12, 1942, "I hope I will be able to confide everything to you,
as I have never been able to confide in anyone, and I hope you'll
be a great source of comfort and support."

No one could have anticipated just how much comfort and
support she'd need. Twenty-four days after that first entry, Anne
and her Jewish family were forced into hiding, in the cramped

attic annex over her father's warehouse in Amsterdam. It's where they would spend the next two years, hoping the Nazis would not discover them.

Anne Frank had wanted a diary for understandable reasons. She was a teenager. She had been lonely, scared, and bored before, but now she was cooped up in a set of cramped, suffocating rooms with six other people. It was all so overwhelming, all so unfair and unfamiliar. She needed somewhere to put those feelings.

According to her father, Otto, Anne didn't write every day, but she always wrote when she was upset or dealing with a problem. She also wrote when she was confused, when she was curious. She wrote in that journal as a form of therapy, so as not to unload her troubled thoughts on the family and compatriots with whom she shared such unenviable conditions. One of her best and most insightful lines must have come on a particularly difficult day. "Paper," she said, "has more patience than people."

Anne used her journal to reflect. "How noble and good every one could be," she wrote, "if at the end of the day they were to review their own behavior and weigh up the rights and wrongs. They would automatically try to do better at the start of each new day, and after a while, would certainly accomplish a great deal." She observed that writing allowed her to watch herself as if she were a stranger. At a time when hormones usually make teenagers more selfish, she regularly reviewed her writings to challenge and improve her own thinking. Even with death lurking outside the doors, she worked to make herself a better person.

The list of people, ancient and modern, who practiced the art of journaling is almost comically long and fascinatingly diverse. Among them: Oscar Wilde, Susan Sontag, Marcus Aurelius, Queen Victoria, John Quincy Adams, Ralph Waldo Emerson, Virginia Woolf, Joan Didion, Shawn Green, Mary Chesnut, Brian Koppelman, Anaïs Nin, Franz Kafka, Martina Navratilova, and Ben Franklin.

All journalers.

Some did it in the morning. Some did it sporadically. Some, like Leonardo da Vinci, kept their notebooks on their person at all times. John F. Kennedy kept a diary during his travels before World War II, and then as president was more of a notetaker and a doodler (which is shown in studies to improve memory) on White House stationery both to clarify his thinking and to keep a record of it.

Obviously this is an intimidating list of individuals. But Anne Frank was thirteen, fourteen, and fifteen years old. If she can do it, what excuse do we have?

Seneca, the Stoic philosopher, seems to have done his writing and reflection in the evenings, much along the lines of Anne Frank's practice. When darkness had fallen and his wife had gone to sleep, he explained to a friend, "I examine my entire day and go back over what I've done and said, hiding nothing from myself, passing nothing by." Then he would go to bed, finding that "the sleep which follows this self-examination" was particularly sweet. Anyone who reads him today can feel him reaching for stillness in these nightly writings.

Michel Foucault talked of the ancient genre of *hupomnemata* (notes to oneself). He called the journal a "weapon for spiritual combat," a way to practice philosophy and purge the mind of agitation and foolishness and to overcome difficulty. To silence the barking dogs in your head. To prepare for the day ahead. To reflect on the day that has passed. Take note of insights you've heard. Take the time to feel wisdom flow through your fingertips and onto the page.

This is what the best journals look like. They aren't for the reader. They are for the *writer*. To slow the mind down. To wage peace with oneself.

Journaling is a way to ask tough questions: Where am I standing in my own way? What's the smallest step I can take toward a big thing today? Why am I so worked up about this? What blessings can I count right now? Why do I care so much about impressing people? What is the harder choice I'm avoiding? Do I rule my fears, or do they rule me? How will today's difficulties reveal my character?*

While there are plenty of people who will anecdotally swear to the benefits of journaling, the research is compelling too. According to one study, journaling helps improve well-being after traumatic and stressful events. Similarly, a University of Arizona

---

*Check out *The Daily Stoic Journal,* published by Portfolio, if you're looking for a journal with prompts.

study showed that people were able to better recover from divorce and move forward if they journaled on the experience. Keeping a journal is a common recommendation from psychologists as well, because it helps patients stop obsessing and allows them to make sense of the many inputs—emotional, external, psychological—that would otherwise overwhelm them.

That's really the idea. Instead of carrying that baggage around in our heads or hearts, we put it down on paper. Instead of letting racing thoughts run unchecked or leaving half-baked assumptions unquestioned, we force ourselves to write and examine them. Putting your own thinking down on paper lets you see it from a distance. It gives you objectivity that is so often missing when anxiety and fears and frustrations flood your mind.

What's the best way to start journaling? Is there an ideal time of day? How long should it take?

Who cares?

How you journal is much less important than *why* you are doing it: To get something off your chest. To have quiet time with your thoughts. To clarify those thoughts. To separate the harmful from the insightful.

There's no right way or wrong way. The point is *just to do it.*

If you've started before and stopped, start again. Getting out of the rhythm happens. The key is to carve out the space again, *today.* The French painter Eugène Delacroix—who called Stoicism his consoling religion—struggled as we struggle:

> I am taking up my Journal again after a long break. I
> think it may be a way of calming this nervous excitement
> that has been worrying me for so long.

Yes!

That is what journaling is about. It's spiritual windshield wipers, as the writer Julia Cameron once put it. It's a few minutes of reflection that both demands and creates stillness. It's a break from the world. A framework for the day ahead. A coping mechanism for troubles of the hours just past. A revving up of your creative juices, for relaxing and clearing.

Once, twice, three times a day. Whatever. Find what works for you.

Just know that it may turn out to be the most important thing you do all day.

CULTIVATE SILENCE

> All profound things, and emotions of things are pre-
> ceded and attended by Silence. . . . Silence is the gen-
> eral consecration of the universe.
>
> —HERMAN MELVILLE

The fascination with silence began early in life for the composer John Cage. In 1928, in a speech contest for Los Angeles High School, he tried to persuade his fellow students and the judges that America should institute a national day of quiet. By observing silence, he told the audience, they would finally be able to "hear what other people think."

It was the beginning of Cage's lifelong exploration and experimentation with what it means to be quiet and the opportunities for listening that this disciplined silence creates.

Cage wandered after high school. He toured Europe. He studied painting. He taught music. He composed classical music. He was an avid observer. Born in 1915 in California, he was just old enough to remember what premechanized life was like, and as the century became modern—and technology remade every industry and occupation—he began to notice just how loud everything had become.

"Wherever we are, what we hear is mostly noise," he would say. "When we ignore it, it disturbs us. When we listen to it, we find it fascinating."

To Cage, silence was not necessarily the absence of all sound. He loved the sound of a truck at 50 miles an hour. Static on the radio. The hum of an amplifier. The sound of water on water. Most of all, he appreciated the sounds that were missed or overwhelmed by our noisy lives.

In 1951, he visited an anechoic chamber, the most advanced soundproof room in the world at the time. Even there, with his highly sensitive musician's ear, he heard sounds. Two sounds, one high and one low. Speaking with the engineer afterward, he was amazed to discover that the source of those sounds was his own nervous system and the pumping of his blood.

How many of us have ever come close to this kind of quiet? Reducing the noise and chatter around you to the degree that you can literally hear your own life? Can you imagine? What you could *do* with that much silence!

It was a reaction against unnecessary noise that inspired Cage's most famous creation, *4'33"*, which was originally conceived with the title *Silent Prayer*. Cage wanted to create a song identical to the popular music of the day—it'd be the same length, it'd be performed live and played on the radio like every other song. The only difference was that *4'33"* would be a "piece of un-interrupted silence."

Some people saw this as an absurd joke, a Duchampian send-up of what constitutes "music." In one sense, it was. (Cage thought it would be funny to sell the "song" to Muzak Co. to be played in elevators.) But it was also inspired by his lifelong study of Zen philosophy, a philosophy that finds fullness in emptiness. The performance instructions for the song are themselves a beautiful contradiction: "In a situation provided with maximum amplification, perform a disciplined action."

In fact, *4'33"* was never about achieving perfect silence—it's about what happens when you stop contributing to the noise. The song was first performed at Woodstock, New York, by the pianist David Tudor.* "There's no such thing as silence," Cage said of that first performance. "What they thought was silence, because they didn't know how to listen, was full of accidental sounds. You could hear the wind stirring outside during the first move-ment. During the second, raindrops began pattering the roof, and during the third the people themselves made all kinds of interesting sounds as they talked or walked out."

We were given two ears and only one mouth for a reason, the philosopher Zeno observed. What you'll notice when you stop to listen can make all the difference in the world.

Too much of our lives is defined by noise. Headphones go in (noise-*canceling* headphones so that we can better hear . . .

---

*In 2015, a late-night talk show recorded a version performed by a cat.

noise). Screens on. Phones ringing. The quiet metal womb of a jumbo jet, traveling at 600 miles per hour, is filled with nothing but people trying to avoid silence. They'd rather watch the same bad movies again and again, or listen to some inane interview with an annoying celebrity, than stop and absorb what's happening around them. They'd rather close their mind than sit there and have to use it.

"Thought will not work except in silence," Thomas Carlyle said. If we want to think better, we need to seize these moments of quiet. If we want more revelations—more insights or breakthroughs or new, big ideas—we have to create more room for them. We have to step away from the comfort of noisy distractions and stimulations. We have to start listening.

In downtown Helsinki, there is a small building called the Kamppi Chapel. It's not a place of worship, strictly speaking, but it's as quiet as any cathedral. Quieter, in fact, because there are no echoes. No organs. No enormous creaking doors. It is, in fact, a Church of Silence. It's open to anyone and everyone who is interested in a moment of quiet spirituality in a busy city.

You walk in and there is just silence.

Glorious, sacred silence. The kind of silence that lets you really start *hearing*.

Randall Stutman, who for decades has been the behind-the-scenes advisor for many of the biggest CEOs and leaders on Wall Street, once studied how several hundred senior executives of major corporations recharged in their downtime. The answers were things like sailing, long-distance cycling, listening quietly to classical music, scuba diving, riding motorcycles, and fly-fishing. All these activities, he noticed, had one thing in common: *an absence of voices.*

These were people with busy, collaborative professions. People who made countless high-stakes decisions in the course of a day. But a couple hours without chatter, without other people in their ear, where they could simply think (or not think), they could recharge and find peace. They could be still—even if they were moving. They could finally hear, even if over the sounds of a roaring river or the music of Vivaldi.

Each of us needs to cultivate those moments in our lives. Where we limit our inputs and turn down the volume so that we can access a deeper awareness of what's going on around us. In shutting up—even if only for a short period—we can finally hear what the world has been trying to tell us. Or what we've been trying to tell ourselves.

That quiet is so rare is a sign of its value. Seize it.

We can't be afraid of silence, as it has much to teach us. Seek it.

The ticking of the hands of your watch is telling you how time is passing away, never to return. Listen to it.

SEEK WISDOM

Imperturbable wisdom is worth everything.

—DEMOCRITUS

In Greece in 426 BC, the priestess of Delphi answered a question posed to her by a citizen of Athens: Was there anyone wiser than Socrates?

Her answer: No.

This idea that Socrates could be the wisest of them all was a surprise, to Socrates especially.

Unlike traditionally wise people who knew many things, and unlike pretentious people who claimed to know many things, Socrates was intellectually humble. In fact, he spent most of his life sincerely proclaiming his lack of wisdom.

Yet this was the secret to his brilliance, the reason he has stood apart for centuries as a model of wisdom. Six hundred years after Socrates's death, Diogenes Laërtius would write that what made Socrates so wise was that "he knew nothing except just the fact of his ignorance." Better still, he was aware of what he did *not* know and was always willing to be proven wrong.

Indeed, the core of what we now call the Socratic method comes from Socrates's real and often annoying habit of going around asking questions. He was constantly probing other people's views. *Why do you think that? How do you know? What evidence do you have? But what about this or that?*

This open-minded search for truth, for *wisdom,* was what made Socrates the most brilliant and challenging man in Athens—so much so that they later killed him for it.

All philosophical schools preach the need for wisdom. The Hebrew word for wisdom is חכמה (*chokmâh*); the corresponding term in Islam is *ḥikma,* and both cultures believe that God was an endless source of it. The Greek word for wisdom was *sophia,* which in Latin became *sapientia* (and why man is called *Homo sapiens*). Both the Epicureans and the Stoics held *sophia* up as a core tenet. In their view, wisdom was gained through experience and study. Jesus advised his followers to be as wise as snakes and as innocent as doves. Proverbs 4:7 holds acquiring wisdom to be the most important thing people can do.

The Buddhists refer to wisdom as *prajñā,* and took wisdom to mean the understanding of the true nature of reality. Confucius and his followers spoke constantly of the cultivation of wisdom, saying that it is achieved in the same way that a craftsman develops skill: by putting in the time. Xunzi was more explicit: "Learning must never cease. . . . The noble person who studies widely and examines himself each day will become clear in his knowing and faultless in his conduct."

Each school has its own take on wisdom, but the same themes appear in all of them: The need to ask questions. The need to study and reflect. The importance of intellectual humility. The power of experiences—most of all failure and mistakes—to open our eyes to *truth* and *understanding.* In this way, wisdom is a sense of the big picture, the accumulation of experience and the ability to rise above the biases, the traps that catch lazier thinkers.

The fact that you are sitting here reading a book is a wonderful step on the journey to wisdom. But don't stop here—this book is only an introduction to classical thinking and history. Tolstoy expressed his exasperation at people who didn't read deeply and regularly. "I cannot understand," he said, "how some people can live without communicating with the wisest people who ever lived on earth." There's another line, now cliché, that is even more cutting: People who don't read have no advantage over those who cannot read.

There's little advantage to reading with arrogance or to confirm preexisting opinions either. Hitler, spent his short prison sentence after World War I reading the classics of history. Except instead of learning anything, he found in those thousands of pages only that, as he said, "I recognized the correctness of my views."

That's not wisdom. Or even stupidity. That's insanity.

We must also seek mentors and teachers who can guide us in our journey. Stoicism, for instance, was founded when Zeno, then a successful merchant, first heard someone reading the teachings of Socrates out loud in a bookstore. But that wasn't enough. What he did *next* was what put him on the path to wisdom, for he walked up to the person reading and said, "Where can I find a man like that?" In Buddhism, there is the idea of *pabbajja,* which means "to go forth" and marks the serious beginning of one's studies. That's what Zeno was doing. Answering the call and going forth.

Zeno's teacher was a philosopher named Crates, and Crates not only gave him many things to read, but like all great mentors helped him address personal issues. It was with Crates's help that Zeno overcame his crippling focus on what other people thought of him, in one case by dumping soup on Zeno and pointing out how little anyone cared or even noticed.

Buddha's first teacher was an ascetic named Alara Kalama, who taught him the basics of meditation. When he learned everything he could from Kalama, he moved on to Uddaka Ramaputta, who was also a good teacher. It was during Ramaputta's time that Buddha started to realize the limitations of the existing schools and consider striking out on his own.

If Zeno and Buddha needed teachers to advance, then we will *definitely* need help. And the ability to admit that is evidence of not a small bit of wisdom!

Find people you admire and ask how they got where they are. Seek book recommendations. Isn't that what Socrates would do?

Add experience and experimentation on top of this. Put yourself in tough situations. Accept challenges. Familiarize yourself with the unfamiliar. That's how you widen your perspective and your understanding. The wise are still because they have *seen it all.* They know what to expect because they've been through so much. They've made mistakes and learned from them. And so must you.

Wrestle with big questions. Wrestle with big ideas. Treat your brain like the muscle that it is. Get stronger through resistance and exposure and training.

Do not mistake the pursuit of wisdom for an endless parade of sunshine and kittens. Wisdom does not immediately produce stillness or clarity. Quite the contrary. It might even make things less clear—make them darker before the dawn.

Remember, Socrates looked honestly at what he didn't know. That's hard. It's painful to have our illusions punctured. It's humbling to learn that we are not as smart as we thought we were.

It's also inevitable that the diligent student will uncover disconcerting or challenging ideas—about the world and about themselves. This will be unsettling. How could it not be?

But that's okay.

It's better than crashing through life (and into each other) like blind moles, to borrow Khrushchev's analogy.

We want to sit with doubt. We want to savor it. We want to follow it where it leads.

Because on the other side is truth.

FIND CONFIDENCE, AVOID EGO

Avoid having your ego so close to your position that
when your position falls, your ego goes with it.

—COLIN POWELL

In 1000 BC in the Valley of Elah, the people of Israel and Philistia were locked in terrible war. No end was in sight until the towering Goliath offered a bold challenge to end the stalemate between the armies. "This day I defy the armies of Israel! Give me a man and let us fight each other," he shouted.

For forty days, not a single soldier stepped forward, not even the king of Israel, Saul. If Goliath was driven by ego and hubris, the Israelites were paralyzed by fear and doubt.

Then came young David, a visiting shepherd with three brothers in the army. David heard Goliath's challenge, and unlike the entire army, cowering in fear, he was *confident* that he could fight Goliath and win. Was he crazy? How could he possibly think he could beat someone so big?

"When a lion or a bear came and carried off a sheep from the flock," David said to his brothers, "I went after it, struck it, and rescued the sheep from its mouth. When it turned on me, I seized it by its hair, struck it, and killed it. Your servant has killed both the lion and the bear; this Philistine will be like one of them."

David's confidence arose from experience, not ego. He had been through worse and done it with his bare hands.

David knew his strengths, but he also knew his weaknesses. "I cannot go in these," he said after trying on a soldier's armor, "because I am not used to them." He was ready to proceed with what we could call true self-awareness (and of course, his faith).

How did Goliath respond to his tiny challenger? Like your typical bully: He laughed. "Am I a dog, that you come at me with sticks?" Goliath shouted. "Come here," he said, "and I'll give your flesh to the birds and the wild animals!"

This arrogance would be short-lived.

David came at Goliath at a full sprint, a sling in one hand and a few stones from the river in the other. In those few quick seconds, Goliath must have seen the confidence in David's eyes and been afraid for the first time—and before he could do anything, he was dead. Felled by the stone flung expertly from David's sling. His head cut off by his own sword.

The story of these two combatants may be true. It may be a fable. But it remains one of the best stories we have about the perils of ego, the importance of humility, and the necessity of confidence.

There is perhaps no one less at peace than the egomaniac, their mind a swirling miasma of their own grandiosity and insecurity. They constantly bite off more than they can chew. They pick fights everywhere they go. They create enemies. They are incapable of learning from their mistakes (because they don't believe they make any). Everything with them is complicated, everything is *about* them.

Life is lonely and painful for the man or woman driven by ego. Donald Trump in the White House at night, his wife and son far away, in his bathrobe, ranting about the news. Alexander the Great, drunk again, fighting and killing his best friend over a stupid argument, thinking of nothing but the next conquest. Howard Hughes, trapped in his mansion, manically excited about some crazy project (which he will inevitably sabotage).

Successful, yes, but would you want to trade places with them?

This toxic form of ego has a less-assuming evil twin—often called "imposter syndrome."

It's a nagging, endless anxiety that you're not qualified for what you're doing—and you're about to be found out for it. Shakespeare's image for this feeling was of a thief wearing a stolen robe he knows is too big. The writer Franz Kafka, the son of an overbearing and disapproving father, likened imposter syndrome to the feeling of a bank clerk who is cooking the books. Frantically trying to keep it all going. Terrified of being discovered.

Of course, this insecurity exists almost entirely in our heads.

People aren't thinking about you. They have their own problems to worry about!

What is better than these two extremes—ego and imposter syndrome—but simple confidence? Earned. Rational. Objective. *Still.*

Ulysses S. Grant had an egotistical, self-promoting father, who was always caught up in some scheme or scandal. Grant knew that wasn't who he wanted to be. In response, he developed a cool and calm self-confidence that was much closer to his mother's quiet but strong personality. It was the source of his greatness.

Before the Civil War, Grant experienced a long chain of setbacks and financial difficulties. He washed up in St. Louis, selling firewood for a living—a hard fall for a graduate of West Point. An army buddy found him and was aghast. "Great God, Grant, what are you doing?" he asked. Grant's answer was simple: "I am solving the problem of poverty."

That's the answer of a confident person, a person at peace even in difficulty. Grant wouldn't have chosen this situation, but he wasn't going to let it affect his sense of self. Besides, he was too busy trying to fix it where he could. Why hate himself for working for a living? What was shameful about that?

Observers often commented on Grant's unshakable confidence in battle. When other generals were convinced that defeat was imminent, Grant never was. He knew he just needed to stay the course. He also knew that losing hope—or his cool—was unlikely to help anything.

With similar equanimity, he was equally unchanged by his success and power in later years, not just leading a powerful army but spending eight years as a world leader. (Charles Dana observed of Grant that he was an "unpretending hero, whom no ill omens could deject and no triumph unduly exalt.") After his presidency, Grant visited the old cabin where he and his wife had lived in those hard days. One of his aides pointed out what an incredible rags-to-riches story his life was—almost like the plot of an epic poem—to go from that cabin to the presidency. Grant shrugged. "Well I never thought about it in that light."

This is also confidence. Which needs neither congratulations nor glory in which to revel, because it is an honest understanding of our strengths and weakness that reveals the path to a greater glory: inner peace and a clear mind.

Confident people know what matters. They know when to ignore other people's opinions. They don't boast or lie to get ahead (and then struggle to deliver). Confidence is the freedom to set your own standards and unshackle yourself from the need to prove yourself. A confident person doesn't fear disagreement and doesn't see change—swapping an incorrect opinion for a correct one—as an admission of inferiority.

Ego, on the other hand, is unsettled by doubts, afflicted by hubris, exposed by its own boasting and posturing. And yet it will not probe itself—or allow itself to be probed—because it knows what might be found.

But confident people are open, reflective, and able to see

themselves without blinders. All this makes room for stillness, by removing unnecessary conflict and uncertainty and resentment.

And you? Where are you on this spectrum?

There are going to be setbacks in life. Even a master or a genius will experience a period of inadequacy when they attempt to learn new skills or explore new domains. Confidence is what determines whether this will be a source of anguish or an enjoyable challenge. If you're miserable every time things are not going your way, if you cannot enjoy it when things *are* going your way because you undermine it with doubts and insecurity, life will be hell.

And sure, there is no such thing as full confidence, or ever-present confidence. We will waver. We will have doubts. We will find ourselves in new situations of complete uncertainty. But still, we want to look inside that chaos and find that kernel of calm confidence. That was what Kennedy did in the Cuban Missile Crisis. He had been in tough situations before, like when his PT boat sank in the Pacific and all appeared to be lost. He learned then that panic solved nothing, and that salvation rarely came from rash action. He also learned that he could count on himself and that he could get through it—if he kept his head. Whatever happened, he told himself early in the crisis, no one would write *The Guns of October* about his handling of it. That was something he could control, and so in that he found confidence.

This is key. Both egotistical and insecure people make their flaws central to their identity—either by covering them up or by brooding over them or externalizing them. For them stillness is impossible, because stillness can only be rooted in strength.

That's what we have to focus on.

Don't feed insecurity. Don't feed delusions of grandeur.

Both are obstacles to stillness.

Be confident. You've earned it.

LET GO

Work done for a reward is much lower than work done in the Yoga of wisdom. Set thy heart upon thy work, but never on its reward. Work not for the reward; but never cease to do thy work.

—THE BHAGAVAD GITA

The great archery master Awa Kenzo did not focus on teaching technical mastery of the bow. He spent almost no time instructing his students on how to deliberately aim and shoot, telling them to simply draw a shot back until it "fell from you like ripe fruit."

He preferred instead to teach his students an important mental skill: detachment. "What stands in your way," Kenzo once told his student Eugen Herrigel, "is that you have too much willful will." It was this willful will—the desire to be in control and to dictate the schedule and the process of everything we're a part of—that held Herrigel back from learning, from *really* mastering the art he pursued.

What Kenzo wanted students to do was to put the thought of hitting the target out of their minds. He wanted them to detach even from the idea of an outcome. "The hits on the target," he would say, "are only the outward proof and confirmation of your purposelessness at its highest, of your egolessness, your self-abandonment, or whatever you like to call this state."

That state is *stillness*.

But detachment and purposelessness don't exactly sound like productive attitudes, do they? That was exactly the kind of vexing predicament Kenzo wanted to put his students in. Most of his pupils, like us, wanted to be told what to do and shown how to do it. We're supposed to care, *a lot*. Willful will should be a *strength*. That's what's worked for us since we were kids who wanted to excel in school. How can you improve without it? How can this be the way to hitting a bull's-eye?

Well, let's back up.

Have you ever noticed that the more we want something, the more insistent we are on a certain outcome, the more difficult it can be to achieve it? Sports like golf and archery are the perfect examples of this. When you try to hit the ball *really* hard, you end up snap-hooking it. If you look up to follow the ball, you jerk the club and slice it into the woods. The energy you're spending aiming the arrow—particularly early on—is energy *not* spent developing your form. If you're too conscious of the technical components of shooting, you won't be relaxed or smooth enough. As marksmen say these days, "Slow is smooth, smooth is fast."

Stillness, then, is actually a way to superior performance. Looseness will give you more control than gripping tightly—to a method or a specific outcome.

Obviously an archery master like Kenzo realized that by the early twentieth century the skills he was teaching were no longer matters of life and death. Nobody needed to know how to shoot an arrow for survival. But other skills required to master archery remained essential: focus, patience, breathing, persistence, clarity. And most of all, the ability to let go.

What we need in life, in the arts, in sports, is to loosen up, to become flexible, to get to a place where there is nothing in our way—including our own obsession with certain outcomes. An actor doesn't become his character by *thinking* about it; he has to let go, dispense with technique and sink into the role. Entrepreneurs don't walk the streets deliberately looking for opportunities—they have to open themselves up to noticing the little things around them. The same goes for comedians or even parents trying to raise a good kid.

"Everyone tries to shoot naturally," Kenzo wrote, "but nearly all practitioners have some kind of strategy, some kind of shallow, artificial, calculating technical trick that they rely on when they shoot. Technical tricks ultimately lead nowhere."

Mastering our mental domain—as paradoxical as it might seem—requires us to step back from the rigidity of the word "mastery." We'll get the stillness we need if we focus on the individual steps, if we embrace the process, and give up *chasing*. We'll think better if we aren't thinking so *hard*.

Most students, whether it's in archery or yoga or chemistry, go into a subject with a strong intention. They are outcome-focused. They want to get the best grade or the highest score. They bring their previous "expertise" with them. They want to skip the unnecessary steps and get right to the sexy stuff. As a result, they are difficult to teach and easily discouraged when the journey proves harder than expected. They are not present. They are not open to experience and cannot learn.

In Kenzo's school, it was only when a student had fully surrendered, when they had detached themselves from even the idea of aiming, having spent months firing arrows into a hay bale just a few feet in front of them, that he would finally announce, "Our new exercise is shooting at a target." And even then, when they would hit the target, Kenzo wouldn't shower the archer with praise.

On the contrary, after a bull's-eye, Kenzo would urge them to "go on practicing as if nothing happened." He'd say the same after a bad shot. When the students asked for extra instruction, he'd reply, "Don't ask, *practice!*"

He wanted them to get lost in the process. He wanted them to give up their notions of what archery was supposed to look like. He was demanding that they be present and empty and open—so they could *learn*.

In Hinduism, Buddhism, Sikhism, and Jainism, the lotus

flower is a powerful symbol. Although it rises out of the mud of a pond or a river, it doesn't reach up towering into the sky—it floats freely, serenely on top of the water. It was said that wherever Buddha walked, lotus flowers appeared to mark his footprints. In a way, the lotus also embodies the principle of letting go. It's beautiful and pure, but also attainable and lowly. It is simultaneously attached and detached.

This is the balance we want to strike. If we aim for the trophy in life—be it recognition or wealth or power—we'll miss the target. If we aim too intensely for the target—as Kenzo warned his students—we will neglect the process and the art required to hit it. What we should be doing is practicing. What we should be doing is pushing away that willful will.

The closer we get to mastery, the less we care about specific results. The more collaborative and creative we are able to be, the less we will tolerate ego or insecurity. The more at peace we are, the more productive we can be.

Only through stillness are the vexing problems solved. Only through reducing our aims are the most difficult targets within our reach.

ON TO WHAT'S NEXT . . .

> If the mind is disciplined, the heart turns quickly
> from fear to love.
>
> —JOHN CAGE

The stakes of what each of us is trying to do are too high to allow ourselves to be riven by the chatter of the news or the noise of the crowd. The insights we seek are often buried and rarely obvious—to find them, we need to be able to look deeply, to perceive what others are unable to.

So we ignore the noise. We zero in on what's essential. We sit with presence. We sit with our journals. We empty our minds.

We try, in the words of Marcus Aurelius, to "shrug it all off and wipe it clean—every annoyance and distraction—and reach utter stillness." To build a kind of mental vault or stronghold that no distraction or false impression can breach. For brief moments, we are able to get there. And when we're there, we find ourselves capable of things we didn't even know were possible: Superior performance. Awesome clarity. Profound happiness.

Yet that stillness is often fleeting. Why?

Because it is undermined by disturbances elsewhere—not just the expected turbulence of the surrounding world, but also inside us. In our spirit and our physical bodies.

"The mind tends toward stillness," Lao Tzu said, "but is opposed by craving." We are like the audience at Marina Abramović's performance. Present for a moment. Moved to stillness for a moment. Then back out into the city, back to the old routines and pulled by endless desires and bad habits, as if that experience never happened.

A flash of stillness is not what we're after. We want consistent focus and wisdom that can be called upon in even the most trying situations. Getting there will require more work. It's going to require some holistic self-examination, treating the disease and not just the symptoms.

The premise of this book is that our three domains—the mind, the heart, and the body—must be in harmony. The truth is that for most people not only are these domains out of sync, but they are at war with each other. We will never have peace until that civil war Dr. King described is settled.

History teaches us that peace is what provides the opportunity to build. It is the postwar boom that turns nations into superpowers, and ordinary people into powerhouses.

And so we must go onward to fight the next battle, to pacify the domain of the spirit and purify our hearts, our emotions, our drives, our passions.

PART II

MIND ✦ **SPIRIT** ✦ BODY

Most of us would be seized with fear if our bodies went numb, and would do everything possible to avoid it, yet we take no interest at all in the numbing of our souls.

—EPICTETUS

THE DOMAIN OF THE SOUL

In retrospect, it was one of the finest moments in golf, perhaps in all of sports. In June 2008, Tiger Woods birdied the final hole of the U.S. Open at Torrey Pines, just north of San Diego, to force an eighteen-hole playoff. He took an early three-stroke lead but surrendered it, only to come charging back, to birdie again and force forty-six-year old Rocco Mediate into a head-to-head, sudden-death round. On that 488-yard par-four, Tiger Woods would birdie a final time to win his third U.S. Open and his fourteenth major. The second most major victories in the history of the game.

And Woods was certainly the first person and likely the last golfer in history to win such a roller-coaster match on a torn ACL and a leg *broken* in two places. To call it a triumph of grit and determination almost undersells Woods's performance, because he did it with such poise that no one watching even knew the extent of his injuries.

Woods himself knew only of the fractures, not the fact that his knee joint was basically gone. Yet somehow, with nearly inhuman mental and physical discipline, he transcended every limit the complex and crushing game of golf had tried to place on him, and he did it with little more than an occasional grimace.

We could call this moment the high-water mark of Tiger Woods's career. He took a six-month leave to recover from emergency knee surgery. Not long after, his mistress, Rachel Uchitel, was caught at his hotel in Australia, and suddenly the secrets of his personal life were no longer secret.

When he was confronted by his wife, Tiger tried to lie his way out of it, but the lies stopped working. Within minutes, Tiger was sprawled out in a neighbor's driveway, his SUV crashed into a nearby fire hydrant and the back windows smashed by a golf club. Unconscious, his wife weeping over him, he was, for a moment, *still,* in a way he had not been perhaps since he was a baby.

It did not last long.

The tabloid nightmare of all tabloid nightmares would ensue— twenty-one consecutive covers of the *New York Post*. The text messages. The affairs with porn stars and Perkins waitresses, frantic sex in church parking lots, sex even with the twenty-one-year-old daughters of family friends, all made public. The stint in sex rehab, the loss of his sponsors, and the $100 million divorce—it all nearly broke him, as it would break anyone.

He wouldn't win another major for a decade.

"On the surface of the ocean there is stillness," the monk Thich Nhat Hanh has said of the human condition, "but underneath there are currents." So it was for Tiger Woods. This man who had become an icon for his ability to be calm and focused in moments of intense stress, a man with the physical discipline to pump the emergency brake on his 129-mile-per-hour swing if he wanted to start over, the champion of the "stillest" of sports, was at the mercy of insatiable riptides that lurked beneath his placid demeanor. And as any seasoned captain of the seas of life can tell you, what's happening on the surface of the water doesn't matter—it's what's going on below that will kill you.

Tiger Woods could stare down opponents and unimaginable pressure, persevere through the countless obstacles in his career. He just couldn't do the same for his own spiritual demons.

The seeds of Tiger's undoing were sown early. His father, Earl, was a complicated man. Born into poverty, Earl Woods lived through the worst of American racism and segregation. He managed to put himself through college and join the army, where he became a Green Beret in Vietnam. Beneath the surface of this accomplishment there were also currents—of narcissism, egotism, dishonesty, and greed. A simple example: Earl Woods returned from his second tour in Vietnam with a new wife . . . a fact he neglected to mention to the wife and three children he already had.

When Tiger was born of that second marriage, Earl Woods was forty-three years old and not particularly excited to become a father again. For the first year of Tiger's life, fatherhood mostly involved strapping the baby in a high chair while hitting golf balls in the garage. It was in fact in watching his father play golf—instead of being able to play like a regular kid—that Tiger developed his almost unnatural obsession with the game. According to family legend, at nine months old Tiger slid down from his chair, picked up a club, and hit a golf ball.

It's a story that is both cute and utterly abnormal. At age two, Tiger Woods appeared on *The Mike Douglas Show* to show off his golf skills. The audience loved it, but Jimmy Stewart, the other guest that day, was not amused. "I've seen too many precious kids like this sweet little boy," he told Douglas backstage, "and too many starry-eyed parents."

Still, his parents' dedication is undoubtedly what allowed Tiger Woods to become a great golfer. Thousands of hours in the garage watching his father hit seared the beautiful mechanics of a swing into his mind. The thousands more hours they spent at the driving range and playing golf—thanks in part to the discounted rates Earl Woods got at the military course near their home—were instrumental. His parents sacrificed for him, drove him to tournaments, and hired the best coaches.

They didn't stop there. Earl Woods knew that golf was a mental game, so he worked to prepare his son for the unforgiving world of sports. Starting when Tiger was about seven, Earl took active measures to develop his son's concentration. Whenever Tiger teed off, Earl would cough. Or jingle change in his pocket. Or drop his clubs. Or throw a ball at him. Or block his line of sight. "I wanted to teach him mental toughness," Earl recounted. "If he got distracted by the little things I did, he'd never be able to handle the pressure of a tournament."

But as Tiger got older, the training became, even by Earl's admission, an increasingly brutal finishing school. It was a boot camp of "prisoner-of-war interrogation techniques" and "psychological intimidation" that no civilized person ought to inflict on another. "He constantly put me down," Tiger said later. "He would push me to the breaking point, then back off. It was wild."

Yeah. *Wild.*

That's what it is for a child to hear his father taunt him as he tries to play a sport, to call him a "motherfucker" while he's trying to concentrate. Imagine how painful it would be to have your dad tell you to "fuck off," or to ask, "How do you feel being a little nigger?" to try to get a rise out of you. Earl Woods even cheated when they played together, supposedly to keep his son humble and on his game. As Tiger reflected, this was all deliberate training to become what his father wanted him to be: a "'cold-blooded assassin' on the course."

Now, Tiger, who clearly loved his father, said that they had a code word he could use if his father ever pushed too far—in either their mental or physical training—and that all Tiger had to do was say it and Earl would stop. Tiger says he never did, because he needed and enjoyed the training, but even the word itself is illustrative. It wasn't a cute inside joke or some silly word that meant nothing. The word that Tiger could utter to get his father to stop bullying him, to get him to treat him like a normal child, was, if you can believe it: *enough.*

And not only was it never uttered, but the two of them came to refer to it almost as an expletive: the "e-word."

The e-word was something quitters said, that only losers believed in.

Are we surprised, then, that this talented boy would go on to win so much? But that those wins didn't make him happy? He was imperturbable on the golf course and utterly miserable inside.

Tiger's mother taught him lessons too. She told him, "You will never, ever ruin my reputation as a parent because I will beat you." Notice the threat of physical violence and what it was over—not doing *wrong* but *embarrassing* her. Earl Woods, as a husband, showed Tiger early on how to balance this razor's edge too. He cheated on his wife when he traveled with his son. He drank to excess. He even, likely in violation of amateur sporting rules, accepted a secret $50,000-a-year stipend from IMG, the sports agency that would eventually represent Tiger Woods.

The lesson there? Appearances are the only thing that matters. Do whatever it takes to win—just don't get caught.

A less talented and dedicated athlete would have been crippled by this abuse. But Tiger Woods was not just naturally gifted, he truly loved golf and he loved the work of it. So he got better and better.

By the time he was three, he was beating ten-year-olds. By eleven years old, he could beat his father regularly on eighteen-hole courses. By seventh grade, he was being recruited by Stanford. At Stanford, where he spent two years, Tiger was an All-American and the number one player in the country. By the time he went pro at twenty, it was already obvious that he might become the greatest golfer who ever lived. The richest too. His first contracts with Nike and Titleist were worth a combined $60 million.

Tiger Woods's first decade and a half as a pro stand as possibly the most dominant reign ever, in any sport. He won everything that could be won. Fourteen majors, 140 tournaments. He was ranked the number one golfer in the world for *281 consecutive weeks*. He won more than $115 million in PGA Tour winnings. He won on every continent except Antarctica.

There were, for those who were looking, signs of sickness: the thrown clubs after a bad hole—and the lack of concern for the fans this occasionally imperiled. The way he'd broken up with his longtime high school girlfriend by packing her suitcase and sending it to her parents' hotel room with a letter. The way he responded when Steve Scott saved him from accidentally scratching in their epic head-to-head match, not even thanking him, not even acknowledging the incredible sportsmanship of it—treating it like the weakness of inferior prey.* The way he'd left his college golf team to go pro without even saying goodbye to his teammates, the way after he finished eating with family or friends he'd simply get up and leave without saying a word. The way he could just cut people out of his life.

Woods's golf coach Hank Haney would say that over time Tiger began to understand that "anyone who was brought into his world was lucky and would be playing by his rules." This was

---

*After the match, Steve Scott would marry his caddy and they would live happily ever after.

what he had been taught by his parents, who raised him both as a kind of prince and a prisoner in a psychological experiment. Fame and wealth only added to this. "I felt I had worked hard my entire life and deserved to enjoy all the temptations around me," Tiger would say later. "I felt I was entitled. Thanks to money and fame, I didn't have to go far to find them."

We can imagine Tiger Woods, like so many successful people, getting less happy the more he achieved. Less freedom. Less and less sleep, until it came only with medication. Even with a beautiful, brilliant wife whom he loved, even with two children, whom he also loved, even as the undisputed champion of his craft, he was miserable, tortured by a spiritual malady and a crushing anxiety from which there was no relief.

His mind was strong but his soul ached. It ached over his tragic relationship with his father. It ached over the childhood he had lost. It ached because it *ached—Why am I not happy,* he must have thought, *don't I have everything I ever wanted?*

It's not simply that Tiger loved to win. It's that for so long winning was not nearly enough and never could be enough (the *e*-word). He would tell Charlie Rose, "Winning was fun. Beating someone's even better." Tiger said this *after* his public humiliation, after his multiyear slump, after his stint in sex rehab. He still had not learned. He still could not see what this attitude had cost him.

Everybody's got a hungry heart—that's true. But how we choose to feed that heart matters. It's what determines the kind of person we end up being, what kind of trouble we'll get into, and whether we'll ever be *full,* whether we'll ever really be still.

When Tiger Woods's father died in 2006, Tiger's extramarital affairs went into overdrive. He spent time in clubs, partying, instead of at home with his family. His behavior on the course grew worse, more standoffish, angrier. He also began to spend unusual amounts of time with Navy SEALS, indulging in an impossible fantasy that he might quit golf and join the Special Forces, despite being in his early thirties (and one of the most famous people in the world). In one weekend in 2007, Tiger Woods reportedly jumped out of a plane ten times. In fact, the injuries that plague him to this day are likely a result of that training, not golf—including an accident where his knee was kicked out from under him in a military exercise "clearing" a building.

There he was—rather than enjoying his wealth, success, and family—cheating on his wife, playing a soldier in some sort of early midlife crisis. "Mirror, mirror on the wall, we grow up like our daddy after all," a friend of Earl and Tiger's would say of the situation. Like so many of us, Tiger had unconsciously replicated the most painful and worst habits of his parents.

Some have looked at those fruitless years after Tiger's return to golf as evidence that the selfishness of his previous life helped his game. Or that somehow the work he did in rehab opened up wounds better left bound up.

As if Tiger Woods, a *human being,* did not deserve happiness and existed solely to win trophies and entertain us on television. "For what is a man profited," Jesus asked his disciples, "if he shall gain the whole world, and lose his own soul?"

It's a question we must ask ourselves. Cheating and lying never helped anyone in the long run, whether it was done at work or at home. In Tiger's case, it was that he was so talented, he could get away with it . . . until he couldn't.

Eventually one has to say the e-word, *enough*. Or the world says it for you.

In one sense, his father's training had succeeded. Tiger Woods was mentally tough. He was cold-blooded and talented. But in every other part of his life, he was weak and fragile—bankrupt and unbalanced. That stillness existed only on the golf course; everywhere else he was at the mercy of his passions and urges. As he worked to crowd out distractions—anything that would get in the way of his concentration addressing each shot—he was also crowding out so many other essential elements of life: An open heart. Meaningful relationships. Selflessness. Moderation. A sense of right and wrong.

These are not just important elements of a balanced life; they are sources of stillness that allow us to endure defeat and enjoy victory. Mental stillness will be short-lived if our hearts are on fire, or our souls ache with emptiness. We are incapable of seeing what is essential in the world if we are blind to what's going on within us. We cannot be in harmony with anyone or anything if the need for more, more, more is gnawing at our insides like a maggot.

"When you live a life where you're lying all the time, life is no fun," Tiger would say later. When your life is out of balance, it's not fun. When your life is solely and exclusively about yourself, it's worse than not fun—it's empty and awful. Tiger Woods wasn't just a solitary man; he was, like so many of us in the modern world, *an island*. He might have been famous, but he was a stranger to himself. No one who reads about his endless affairs gets the sense that he was enjoying it or that they brought him much pleasure. In fact, it almost feels like he wanted to get caught. So he could get help.

We don't need to judge Tiger Woods. We need to learn from him, from both his fall and his long and valiant journey back to winning the Masters in 2019 at forty-three years old with a fused back, with his own young son cheering him on. Because we share the same flaws, the same weaknesses—and have the same potential for greatness, if we are willing to put in the work.

Marcus Aurelius would ask himself, "What am I doing with my soul? Interrogate yourself, to find out what inhabits your so-called mind and what kind of soul you have now. A child's soul? An adolescent's? . . . A tyrant's soul? The soul of a predator—or its prey?"

We need to ask ourselves these questions, too, especially as we become successful.

One of the best stories in Zen literature is a series of ten poems about a farmer and his trouble with a bull. The poems are an allegory about conquering the self, and the titles of each one map out the journey that each of us must go on: We search for the bull, we track the footprints, we find it, we catch it, we tame it, we ride it home.

At first the beast is untamable, it's wild and impossible to contain. But the message is that with struggle and perseverance, with self-awareness and patience—with *enlightenment,* really— eventually we can tame the emotions and the drives inside us. As one of the poems reads:

> *Being well-trained, he becomes*
> *naturally gentle.*
> *Then, unfettered, he obeys his master.*

The narrator is in a state of serenity and peace. He has tamed his wild spirit.

That's what we're trying to do. Since ancient times, people have strived to train and control the forces that reside deep inside them so that they can find serenity, so that they can preserve and protect their accomplishments. What good is it to be rational at work if our personal lives are a hot-blooded series of disasters? How long can we keep the two domains separate anyway? You might rule cities or a great empire, but if you're not in control of yourself, it is all for naught.

The work we must do next is less cerebral and more spiritual. It's work located in the *heart* and in the *soul,* and not in the mind. Because it is our soul that is the key to our happiness (or our unhappiness), contentment (or discontent), moderation (or gluttony), and stillness (or perturbation).

That is why those who seek stillness must come to . . .

- Develop a strong moral compass.
- Steer clear of envy and jealousy and harmful desires.
- Come to terms with the painful wounds of their child-hood.
- Practice gratitude and appreciation for the world around them.
- Cultivate relationships and love in their lives.
- Place belief and control in the hands of something larger than themselves.
- Understand that there will never be "enough" and that the unchecked pursuit of more ends only in bank-ruptcy.

Our soul is where we secure our happiness and unhappiness, contentment or emptiness—and ultimately, determine the extent of our greatness.

We must maintain a good one.

CHOOSE VIRTUE

The essence of greatness is the perception that virtue
is enough.

—RALPH WALDO EMERSON

Marcus Aurelius famously described a number of what he
called "epithets for the self." Among his were: Upright.
Modest. Straightforward. Sane. Cooperative. These were, then,
the traits that served him well as emperor.

There are many other traits that could be added to this list:
Honest. Patient. Caring. Kind. Brave. Calm. Firm. Generous. For-
giving. Righteous.

There is one word, however, under which all these epithets
sit: virtue.

Virtue, the Stoics believed, was the highest good—the *sum-
mum bonum*—and should be the principle behind all our actions.
Virtue is not holiness, but rather moral and civic excellence in

the course of daily life. It's a sense of pure rightness that emerges from our souls and is made real through the actions we take.

The East prized virtue as much as the West. *The Daodejing,* for instance, actually translates as *The Way of Virtue.* Confucius, who advised many of the rulers and princes of his day, would have agreed with Marcus that a leader was well served by the pursuit of virtue. His highest compliment would have been to call a ruler a *junzi*—a word that translators still have trouble finding equivalents for in English but is roughly understood as a person who emanates integrity, honor, and self-control.

If the concept of "virtue" seems a bit stuffy to you, consider the evidence that a virtuous life is worthwhile for *its own sake.* No one has less serenity than the person who does not know what is right or wrong. No one is more exhausted than the person who, because they lack a moral code, must belabor every decision and consider every temptation. No one feels worse about themselves than the cheater or the liar, even if—often especially if—they are showered with rewards for their cheating and lying. Life *is* meaningless to the person who decides their choices have no meaning.

Meanwhile, the person who knows what they value? Who has a strong sense of decency and principle and behaves accordingly? Who possesses easy moral self-command, who leans comfortably upon this goodness, day in and day out? This person has found stillness.

A sort of soul power they can draw on when they face challenges, stress, even scary situations.

Look at the response of Canadian politician Jagmeet Singh to an angry protester during a campaign stop. When the agitated woman came up and started shouting at him about Islam (despite the fact that he is Sikh), he replied with two of his own epithets for the self: "Love and courage." Soon, the crowd began to chant along with him: "Love and courage. Love and courage. Love and courage."

He could've stood there and yelled back. He could have run away. It could have made him cruel and mean, in the moment or forever after. He may well have been prodded in those directions. But instead he remained cool, and those two words helped him recenter in the midst of what not only was a career-on-the-line situation, but probably felt like a life-threatening one.

Different situations naturally call for different virtues and different epithets for the self. When we're going into a tough assignment, we can say to ourselves over and over again, "Strength and courage." Before a tough conversation with a significant other: "Patience and kindness." In times of corruption and evil: "Goodness and honesty."

The gift of free will is that in this life we can choose to be good or we can choose to be bad. We can choose what standards to hold ourselves to and what we will regard as important, honorable, and admirable. The choices we make in that regard determine whether we will experience peace or not.

Which is why each of us needs to sit down and examine ourselves. What do we stand for? What do we believe to be essential and important? What are we really *living* for? Deep in the marrow of our bones, in the chambers of our heart, we know the answer. The problem is that the busyness of life, the realities of pursuing a career and surviving in the world, come between us and that self-knowledge.

Confucius said that virtue is a kind of polestar. It not only provides guidance to the navigator, but it attracts fellow travelers too. Epicurus, who has been unfairly branded by history as a hedonist, knew that virtue was the way to tranquility and happiness. In fact, he believed that virtue and pleasure were two sides of the same coin. As he said:

> It is impossible to live the pleasant life without also living sensibly, nobly, and justly, and conversely it is impossible to live sensibly, nobly, and justly without living pleasantly. A person who does not have a pleasant life is not living sensibly, nobly, and justly, and conversely the person who does not have these virtues cannot live pleasantly.

Where virtue is, so too are happiness and beauty.

Confucius wrote that the "gentleman is self-possessed and relaxed, while the petty man is perpetually full of worry." It's worth a look at Seneca, another Stoic philosopher, who, like Marcus, made his living in politics. Like us, Seneca was full of contradictions. On the one hand, his writings contain some of the most beautiful meditations on morality and self-discipline ever written, and they are obviously the result of incredible concentration and mental clarity. On the other, Seneca was a striver—an ambitious writer-politician who aspired to be re-membered as much for his prose as for his policies.

At the height of his career, he could be found working as a fixer for the emperor, Nero. Nero, although he had begun as a promising student of Seneca, did not make his teacher's job easy. He was deranged, selfish, distractible, paranoid, and coldhearted. Imagine that you spend your evenings writing about the importance of doing the right thing, of temperance and wisdom, and then by day you have to help your all-powerful boss justify trying to assassinate his mother. Seneca knew he should walk away; he probably wanted to, but he never did.

What is virtue? Seneca would ask. His answer: "True and steadfast judgment." And from virtue comes good decisions and happiness and peace. It emanates from the soul and directs the mind and the body.

Yet when we look at Seneca's life, we get the sense that he was the type of man whose ambition did not provide much peace, but instead skewed his decision making. Seneca wrote eloquently of the meaninglessness of wealth, yet came to possess an enormous fortune through questionable means. He believed in mercy, kindness, and compassion, but he willingly served two different emperors who were probably psychopaths. It was as if he didn't believe in his own philosophy enough to put it wholly into practice—he couldn't quite accept that virtue would provide enough to live on.

Money, power, fame just seemed a little more urgent.

Seneca knew of the virtuous path, but chased the prizes that drew him away from it. This choice cost him many sleepless nights and forced him into ethically taxing dilemmas. In the end, it cost him his life. In AD 65, Nero turned on his former teacher and forced him to commit suicide—the evil Seneca had rationalized for so long, it eventually cost him everything.

There's no question it's possible to get ahead in life by lying and cheating and generally being awful to other people. This may even be a quick way to the top. But it comes at the expense of not only your self-respect, but your security too.

Virtue, on the other hand, as crazy as it might seem, is a far more attainable and sustainable way to succeed.

How's that? Recognition is dependent on other people. Getting rich requires business opportunities. You can be blocked from your goals by the weather just as easily as you can by a dictator. But virtue? No one can stop you from knowing what's right. Nothing stands between you and it . . . but yourself.

Each of us must cultivate a moral code, a higher standard that we love almost more than life itself. Each of us must sit down and ask: *What's important to me? What would I rather die for than betray? How am I going to live and why?*

These are not idle questions or the banal queries of a personality quiz. We must have the answers if we want the stillness (and the strength) that emerges from the citadel of our own virtue.

It is for the difficult moments in life—the crossroads that

Seneca found himself on when asked to serve Nero—that virtue can be called upon. Heraclitus said that character was fate. He's right. We develop good character, strong epithets for ourselves, so when it counts, we will not flinch.

So that when everyone else is scared and tempted, we will be virtuous.

We will be still.

HEAL THE INNER CHILD

The child is in me still . . . and sometimes not so still.

—FRED ROGERS

There was always something childlike about Leonardo da Vinci. Indeed, this is what made him such a brilliant artist—his mischievousness, his curiosity, his fascination with inventing and creating. But behind this playfulness was a deep sadness, pain rooted in the events of his early life.

Leonardo was born in 1452, an illegitimate son from a prosperous family of notaries. Though in time his father would invite his bastard son to come live with him, and would help secure Leonardo's first artistic apprenticeship, a distance between them never closed.

At the time, it was customary that the oldest son of a prominent tradesman like Leonardo's father would be chosen to take up his father's profession and eventually take over his business. While the notary guild technically did not recognize *non legittimo* heirs, it's surprising that Leonardo's father never even attempted to appear before a local magistrate and present a petition to legitimate his son.

Leonardo's father would go on to have twelve more children, nine of whom were sons. When he died, he left no specific will, an act that for a notary, familiar with the law, meant one thing: He was legally disinheriting Leonardo in favor of his "real" children. As Leonardo's biographer Walter Isaacson would later write, by excluding Leonardo and never fully accepting him, Piero da Vinci's "primary bequest to his son was to give him an insatiable drive for an unconditional patron."

Indeed, all of Leonardo's artistic life exhibits an almost childlike search for love and acceptance from the powerful men he worked for. He devotedly served his first mentor, Andrea del Verrocchio, for more than eleven years—until Leonardo was twenty-five—an incredibly long time for such a prodigal talent (Michelangelo broke out on his own at sixteen). What could have attracted a sweet soul like Leonardo to Cesare Borgia, a murderous psychopath? Borgia was the only patron who was willing to look at and consider Leonardo's military inventions—a longtime passion project. From Milan to France and to the Vatican itself, Leonardo traveled far and wide in his career, looking for the financial support and artistic freedom he thought would make him whole.

Nearly half a dozen times, he uprooted himself and his workshop in a huff, leaving unfinished commissions behind him. Sometimes it was over a slight. Usually it was because the patron couldn't quite be everything Leonardo wanted. The subtext of his angry letters and half-completed work speaks as loudly to us today as any angry teenager: *You're not my dad. You can't tell me what to do. You don't really love me. I'll show you.*

Many of us carry wounds from our childhood. Maybe someone didn't treat us right. Or we experienced something terrible. Or our parents were just a little too busy or a little too critical or a little too stuck dealing with their own issues to be what we needed.

These raw spots shape decisions we make and actions we take—even if we're not always conscious of that fact.

This should be a relief: The source of our anxiety and worry, the frustrations that seem to suddenly pop out in inappropriate situations, the reason we have trouble staying in relationships or ignoring criticism—it isn't us. Well, it is us, just not *adult* us. It's the seven-year-old living inside us. The one who was hurt by Mom and Dad, the sweet, innocent kid who wasn't seen.

Think of Rick Ankiel, one of the greatest natural pitchers to ever play baseball. He had a brutal childhood in the home of an abusive father and a brother who was a drug dealer. His whole life, he stuffed this pain and helplessness down, focusing on his skill on the mound, eventually becoming the minor leagues' top pitching prospect. Then suddenly, just as his career was starting to go well, in the first game of the playoffs in 2000, in front of millions of people, he lost the ability to control his pitches.

What happened? Just days before, his father and brother had gone to jail on drug charges and Rick had been in the courthouse to see them. He'd been running from that pain and that anger for years, until it finally exploded and shattered the delicate balance that pitching required. It took years of work with Harvey Dorfman, a brilliant, patient sports psychologist, to coax his gifts back. And even then only so far. Ankiel would pitch only five more times in his career, none as a starter. The rest of his career he spent in the outfield—mostly in center field, the position farthest away from the mound.

Sigmund Freud himself wrote about how common it is for deficiencies, big and small, at a young age to birth toxic, turbulent attitudes in adulthood. Because we weren't born rich enough, pretty enough, naturally gifted enough, because we weren't appreciated like other children in the classroom, or because we had to wear glasses or got sick a lot or couldn't afford nice clothes, we carry a chip on our shoulder. Some of us are like Richard III, believing that a deformity entitles us to be selfish or mean or insatiably ambitious. As Freud explained, "We all demand reparation for our early wounds to our narcissism," thinking we are owed because we were wronged or deprived. (This was Tiger Woods to the detail.)

It's dangerous business, though, creating a monster to protect your wounded inner child.

The insecure lens. The anxious lens. The persecuted lens. The prove-them-all-wrong lens. The will-you-be-my-father? lens that Leonardo had. These adaptations, developed early on to make sense of the world, don't make our lives easier. On the contrary.

Who can be happy that way? Would you put a nine-year-old in charge of anything stressful or dangerous or important?

The movie producer Judd Apatow has talked about something he realized after a big fight during the filming of one of his movies. For years, he had seen every note the studio or the executives had for him, every attempt at restrictions or influence, as if it were the obnoxious meddling of his parents. Instinctively, emotionally, he had fought and resisted each intervention. *Who are these idiots to tell me what to do? Why are they always trying to boss me around? Why are they so unfair?*

Each of us on occasion has surprised ourself with a strong reaction to someone's innocuous comments, or thrown a fit when some authority figure tried to direct our actions. Or felt the pull of attraction to a type of relationship that never ends well. Or to a type of behavior that we know is wrong. It's almost primal how deep these feelings go—they're rooted in our infancy.

It took therapy and self-reflection (and probably the observations of his wife) for Apatow to understand that the movie studio was *not his parents.* This was a business transaction and a creative discussion, not another instance of a talented boy being bossed around by otherwise absent parents.

But with that realization came stillness, if only because it deintensified arguments at work. Think about it: How much better and less scary life is when we don't have to see it from the perspective of a scared, vulnerable child? How much lighter will our load be if we're not adding extra baggage on top?

It will take patience and empathy and real self-love to heal the wounds in your life. As Thich Nhat Hanh has written:

> After recognizing and embracing our inner child, the third function of mindfulness is to soothe and relieve our difficult emotions. Just by holding this child gently, we are soothing our difficult emotions and we can begin to feel at ease. When we embrace our strong emotions with mindfulness and concentration, we'll be able to see the roots of these mental formations. We'll know where our suffering has come from. When we see the roots of things, our suffering will lessen. So mindfulness recognizes, embraces, and relieves.

Take the time to think about the pain you carry from your early experiences. Think about the "age" of the emotional reactions you have when you are hurt or betrayed or unexpectedly challenged in some way. That's your inner child. They need a hug from you. They need you to say, "Hey, buddy. *It's okay.* I know you're hurt, but I am going to take care of you."

The functional adult steps in to reassert and reassure. To make stillness possible.

We owe it to ourselves as well as to the people in our lives to do this. Each of us must break the link in the chain of what the Buddhists call *samsara,* the continuation of life's suffering from generation to generation.

The comedian Garry Shandling lost his brother, Barry, at

age ten to cystic fibrosis, and was left for the rest of his life at the mercy of his distraught and controlling mother, who was so disturbed by the loss of her older son that she forbade Garry from attending the funeral for fear that he would see her cry.

But one day, as a much older man, Garry wrote in his diary a formula that might help him overcome that pain and not only heal his own inner child but pass on the lesson to the many surrogate children he had as a mentor and elder in show business.* The formula was simple and is key to breaking the cycle and stilling the deep anguish we carry around with us:

Give more.
Give what you didn't get.
Love more.
Drop the old story.

Try it, if you can.

---

*As it happens, Judd Apatow was one of the most successful of these surrogate children.

BEWARE DESIRE

> Every man has a passion gnawing away at the bottom
> of his heart, just as every fruit has its worm.
>
> —ALEXANDRE DUMAS

John F. Kennedy achieved indisputable greatness through stillness in those thirteen fateful days in October 1962. The world is forever in his debt. But we should not allow that shining moment to obscure the fact that, like all of us, he had demons that dogged and haunted him and undermined that same greatness—and as a result, his stillness.

Kennedy grew up in a house where his father often brought his mistresses home for dinner and on family vacations. It was a house where anger and rage were common too. "When I hate some sonofabitch," Joseph Kennedy liked to say, "I hate him until I die." It's probably not a surprise, then, that his young son would develop his own bad habits and wrestle with controlling his urges and appetites.

The first time Kennedy's sex drive got him in trouble was during the early days of World War II, when he began dating Inga Arvad, a beautiful Dutch journalist who many suspected was a Nazi spy. When he was running for president, he had an affair with Judith Exner, who happened to be the girlfriend of Sam Giancana, a Chicago mobster. But instead of suffering any consequences for theses massive lapses of judgment, Kennedy skated away clean each time, a fact that only escalated his risky behavior.

Kennedy was no romantic. Girlfriends would describe his insatiable but joyless sex drive. According to one conquest, sex was "just physical and social activity to him," a way to stave off the boredom, or get a rush. He didn't care about the other person, and in time, he almost didn't care about the pleasure it gave himself either. As Kennedy told the prime minister of Britain in a moment of very uncomfortable honesty, if he went without sex for a few days, he'd get headaches. (His father had told his sons that he couldn't sleep unless he'd "had a lay.") Given Kennedy's terrible back, having sex was probably painful too—but he never let that stop him.

In one shameful moment, as Soviet and American forces teetered on the brink of nuclear war during the Cuban Missile Crisis, Kennedy brought in a nineteen-year-old student from Wheaton College for a rendezvous in a hotel near the White House. Here was a man who had no idea how much longer he would live, who was working with inhuman dedication in that crisis to curb the dangerous impulses of his nation's enemies . . . cheating on his wife, choosing to spend what were potentially his last moments on earth in the sheets with a random girl half his age instead of with his scared and vulnerable family.

That doesn't sound like stillness. It doesn't sound particularly glamorous either.

It sounds like a man who is spiritually broken, at the whims of his worst impulses, unable to think clearly or prioritize. But before we condemn Kennedy as a despicable addict or abuser, we should look at our own failings. Do we not fall prey to various desires in our own personal lives? Do we not know better and do it anyway?

Lust is a destroyer of peace in our lives: Lust for a beautiful person. Lust for an orgasm. Lust for someone other than the one we've committed to be with. Lust for power. Lust for dominance. Lust for other people's stuff. Lust for the fanciest, best, most expensive things that money can buy.

And is this not at odds with the self-mastery we say we want?

A person enslaved to their urges is not free—whether they are a plumber or the president.

How many great men and women end up losing everything—end up, in some cases, literally behind bars—because they freely chose to indulge their endless appetites, whatever they happened to be?

And at least power and sex and attention are pleasurable. The most common form of lust is *envy*—the lust for what other people have, for the sole reason that they have it. Joseph Epstein's brilliant line is: "Of the seven deadly sins, only envy is no fun at all." Democritus, twenty-four hundred years before him: "An envious man pains himself as though he were an enemy."

No one in the sway of envy or jealousy has a chance to think clearly or live peacefully. How can they?

It is an endless loop of misery. We're envious of one person, while they envy somebody else. The factory worker wishes desperately to be a millionaire, the millionaire envies the simple life of the nine-to-five worker. The famous wish they could go back to the private life that so many others would gladly give away; the man or woman with a beautiful partner thinks only of someone a little more beautiful. It's sobering to consider that the rival we're so jealous of may in fact be jealous of us.

There is also a "have your cake and eat it too" immaturity to envy. We don't simply want what other people have—we want to keep everything we have *and* add theirs to it, even if those things are mutually exclusive (and on top of that, we also want them to not have it anymore). But if you had to trade places entirely with the person you envy, if you had to give up your brain, your principles, your proudest accomplishments to live in their life, would you do it? Are you willing to pay the price they paid to get what you covet?

No, you aren't.

Epicurus, again the supposed hedonist, once said that "sex has never benefited any man, and it's a marvel if it hasn't injured him." He came up with a good test anytime he felt himself being pulled by a strong desire: *What will happen to me if I get what I want? How will I feel after?*

Indeed, *most* desires are at their core irrational emotions, and that's why stillness requires that we sit down and dissect them. We want to think ahead to the refractory period, to consider the inevitable hangover before we take a drink. When we do that, these desires lose some of their power.

To the Epicureans real pleasure was about freedom from pain and agitation. If wanting something makes you miserable while you don't have it, doesn't that diminish the true value of the reward? If getting what you "want" has its consequences too, is that really pleasurable? If the same drive that helps you achieve initially also leads you inevitably to overreach or overdo, is it really an advantage?

Those seeking stillness need not become full-fledged ascetics or puritans. But we can take the time to realize how much pull and power desire can have on us, and beyond the momentary pleasure this might provide us, it deprives us of the deeper peace that we seek.

Think about the times when you feel best. It's not when you are pining away. It's not when you get what you pined for either. There is always a tinge of disappointment or loss at the moment of acquisition.

Krishna in the Bhagavad Gita calls desire the "ever-present enemy of the wise . . . which like a fire cannot find satisfaction." The Buddhists personified this demon in the figure of Mara. They said it was Mara who tried to tempt and distract Buddha from the path of enlightenment, from stillness. When Leonardo da Vinci wrote in his notebook about how to portray envy, he said that she should be shown as lean and haggard due to her state of perpetual torment. "Make her heart gnawed by a swelling serpent," he said, "make her ride upon death because Envy never dies." It'd be hard to find a better depiction of lust either, which Leonardo said puts us "on the level of beasts."

None of us are perfect. We have biologies and pathologies that will inevitably trip us up. What we need then is a philosophy and a strong moral code—that sense of virtue—to help us resist what we can, and to give us the strength to pick ourselves back up when we fail and try to do and be better.

We can also rely on tools to help us resist harmful desires. Saint Athanasius of Alexandria wrote in his *Vita Antonii* that one of the benefits of journaling—Confessions, as the Christians called the genre—was that it helped stop him from sinning. By observing and then writing about his own behavior, he was able to hold himself accountable and make himself better:

> Let us each note and write down our actions and impulses of the soul . . . as though we were to report them to each other; and you may rest assured that from utter shame of becoming known we shall stop sinning and entertaining sinful thoughts altogether. . . . Just as we would not give ourselves to lust within sight of each other, so if we were to write down our thoughts as if telling them to each other, we shall so much the more guard ourselves against foul thoughts for shame of being known. Now, then, let the written account stand for the

eyes of our fellow ascetics, so that blushing at writing the same as if we were actually seen, we may never ponder evil.

To have an impulse and to resist it, to sit with it and examine it, to let it pass by like a bad smell—this is how we develop spiritual strength. This is how we become who we want to be in this world.

Only those of us who take the time to explore, to question, to extrapolate the consequences of our desires have an opportunity to overcome them and to stop regrets before they start. Only they know that real pleasure lies in having a soul that's true and stable, happy and secure.

ENOUGH

History relates no instance in which a conqueror has been surfeited with conquests.

—STEFAN ZWEIG

The writers Kurt Vonnegut, the author of *Slaughterhouse Five,* and Joseph Heller, the author of *Catch-22,* were once at a party in a fancy neighborhood outside New York City. Standing in the palatial second home of some boring billionaire, Vonnegut began to needle his friend. "Joe," he said, "how does it feel that our host only yesterday may have made more money than your novel has earned in its entire history?"

"I've got something he can never have," Heller replied.

"And what on earth could that be?" Vonnegut asked.

"The knowledge that I've got enough."

Earl Woods called that the e-word, like it was an expletive. In truth, *enough* is a beautiful thing.

Imagine the stillness that sense of enough brought Joseph

Heller and everyone else who has it. No ceaseless wanting. No insecurity of comparison. Feeling *satisfied* with yourself and your work? What gift!

Saying the word "enough" is not enough. Deeply spiritual, introspective work is required to understand what that idea means—work that may well destroy illusions and assumptions we have held our entire lives.

John Stuart Mill, the philosopher and boy genius who before he hit puberty read and mastered nearly every major classical text in the original Greek or Latin, is an illustration of just how terrifying this process can be. Extremely driven (by his father and by himself), one day, at around twenty years old, Mill stopped to think, for the first time, about what he was chasing. As he writes:

> It occurred to me to put the question directly to myself, "Suppose that all your objects in life were realized; that all the changes in institutions and opinions which you are looking forward to, could be completely effected at this very instant: would this be a great joy and happiness to you?" And an irrepressible self-consciousness distinctly answered, "No!" At this my heart sank within me: the whole foundation on which my life was constructed fell down.

What ensued was a devastating mental breakdown that required years of recovery. Yet Mill was probably lucky to undergo it so early. Most people *never* learn that their accomplishments will ultimately fail to provide the relief and happiness we tell ourselves they will. Or they come to understand this only after so much time and money, so many relationships and moments of inner peace, were sacrificed on the altar of achievement. We get to the finish line only to think: *This is it? Now what?*

It is a painful crossroads. Or worse, one that we ignore, stuffing those feelings of existential crisis down, piling on top of them meaningless consumption, more ambition, and the delusion that doing more and more of the same will eventually bring about different results.

In a way, this is a curse of one of our virtues. No one achieves excellence or enlightenment without a desire to get better, without a tendency to explore potential areas of improvement. Yet the desire—or the need—for more is often at odds with happiness. Billie Jean King, the tennis great, has spoken about this, about how the mentality that gets an athlete to the top so often prevents them from enjoying the thing they worked so hard for. The need for progress can be the enemy of enjoying the *process.*

There is no stillness for the person who cannot appreciate things as they are, particularly when that person has objectively done so much. The creep of more, more, more is like a hydra. Satisfy one—lop it off the bucket list—and two more grow in its place.

The best insights on *enough* come to us from the East. "When you realize there is nothing lacking," Lao Tzu says, "the whole world belongs to you." The verse in *The Daodejing:*

> *The greatest misfortune is to not know contentment.*
> *The word calamity is the desire to acquire.*
> *And so those who know the contentment of contentment*
>   *are always content.*

The Western philosophers wrestled with the balance between getting more and being satisfied. Epicurus: "Nothing is enough for the man to whom enough is too little." Thomas Traherne: "To have blessings and to prize them is to be in Heaven; to have them and not to prize them is to be in Hell. . . . To prize them and not to have them is to be in Hell." And the Stoics who lived in the material world of an empire at its peak knew the truth about money. Seneca had piles of it and he knew how little it correlated with peace. His work is filled with stories of people who drove themselves to ruin and misery chasing money they didn't need and honors beyond their share.

Temperance. That's the key. Intellectually, we know this. It's only in flashes of insight or tragedy that we *feel* it.

In 2010, Marco Rubio was pacing the halls of his home, making fund-raising calls for his surprise Senate bid, when his three-year-old son snuck out the back door and fell into the pool. Rubio had heard the chime of the door opening, assumed someone else was paying attention, and returned to his important phone call. A few minutes later, he found his son floating facedown in their pool, barely breathing.

Even after this near tragedy he returned almost immediately to work—his ambition, like Lincoln's, a "little engine that knew no rest." Only with distance could Rubio begin to see the cost of this drive, what important things we miss when we give ourselves over to it entirely. As he wrote, "I think I understand now that the restlessness we feel as we make our plans and chase our ambitions is not the effect of their importance to our happiness and our eagerness to attain them. We are restless because deep in our hearts we know now that our happiness is found elsewhere, and our work, no matter how valuable it is to us or to others, cannot take its place. But we hurry on anyway, and attend to our business because we need to matter, and we don't always realize we already do."

Have you ever held a gold medal or a Grammy or a Super Bowl ring? Have you ever seen a bank balance nudging up into the seven figures? Maybe you have, maybe you possess these things yourself. If you do, then you know: They are nice but they change nothing. They are just pieces of metal, dirty paper in your pocket, or plaques on a wall. They are not made of anything strong or malleable enough to plug even the tiniest hole in a person's soul. Nor do they extend the length of one's life even one minute. On the contrary, they may shorten it!

They can also take the joy out of the thing we used to love to do. *More* does nothing for the one who feels *less than,* who cannot see the wealth that was given to them at birth, that they have accumulated in their relationships and experiences. Solving your problem of poverty is an achievable goal and can be fixed by earning and saving money. No one could seriously claim otherwise. The issue is when we think these activities can address *spiritual poverty.*

Accomplishment. Money. Fame. Respect. Piles and piles of them will never make a person feel content.

If you believe there is ever some point where you will feel like you've "made it," when you'll finally be *good,* you are in for an unpleasant surprise. Or worse, a sort of Sisyphean torture where just as that feeling appears to be within reach, the goal is moved just a little bit farther up the mountain and out of reach.

You will never feel okay by way of external accomplishments. *Enough* comes from the inside. It comes from stepping off the train. From seeing what you already have, what you've always had.

If a person can do that, they are richer than any billionaire, more powerful than any sovereign.

Yet instead of seizing this path to power, we choose ingratitude and the insecurity of needing more, more, more. "We are here as if immersed in water head and shoulders underneath the great oceans," said the Zen master Gensha, "and yet how piously we are extending our hands for water." We think we need more and don't realize we already have so much. We work so hard "for our families" that we don't notice the contradiction— that it's because of work that we never see them.

Enough.

Now, there is a perfectly understandable worry that contentment will be the end of our careers—that if we somehow satisfy this urge, all progress in our work and in our lives will come to a screeching halt. *If everyone felt good, why would they keep trying so hard?* First, it must be pointed out that this worry itself is hardly an ideal state of mind. No one does their best work driven by anxiety, and no one should be breeding insecurity in themselves so that they might keep making things. That is not industry, that is slavery.

We were not put on this planet to be worker bees, compelled to perform some function over and over again for the cause of the hive until we die. Nor do we "owe it" to anyone to keep doing, doing, doing—not our fans, not our followers, not our parents who have provided so much for us, not even our families. Killing ourselves does nothing for anybody.

It's perfectly possible to do and make good work from a good place. You can be healthy and still *and* successful.

Joseph Heller believed he had *enough*, but he still kept writing. He wrote six novels after *Catch-22* (when a reporter criticized him by saying he hadn't written anything as good as his first book, Heller replied, "Who has?"), including a number one bestseller. He taught. He wrote plays and movies. He was incredibly productive. John Stuart Mill, after his breakdown, fell in love with poetry, met the woman who would eventually become his wife, and began to slowly return to political philosophy—and ultimately had enormous impact on the world. Indeed, Western democracies are indebted to him for many changes he helped bring about.

The beauty was that these creations and insights came from a better—a *stiller*—place inside both men. They weren't doing it to prove anything. They didn't need to impress anyone. They were in the moment. Their motivations were pure. There was no insecurity. No anxiety. No creeping, painful hope that this would finally be the thing that would make them feel whole, that would give them what they had always been lacking.

What do we want more of in life? That's the question. It's not accomplishments. It's not popularity. It's moments when we feel like we are enough.

More presence. More clarity. More insight. More truth.

More stillness.

BATHE IN BEAUTY

> In the face of the Sublime, we feel a shiver . . . something too large for our minds to encompass. And for a moment, it shakes us out of our smugness and releases us from the deathlike grip of habit and banality.
>
> —ROBERT GREENE

On Wednesday morning, February 23, 1944, Anne Frank climbed up to the attic above the annex where her family had been hiding for two long years to visit Peter, the young Jewish boy who lived with them. After Peter finished his chores, the two of them sat down at Anne's favorite spot on the floor and looked out the small window to the world they had been forced to leave behind.

Staring at the blue sky, the leafless chestnut tree below, birds swooping and diving in the air, the two were entranced to the point of speechlessness. It was so quiet, so serene, so open compared to their cramped quarters.

It was almost as if the world wasn't at war, as if Hitler had not already killed so many millions of people and their families didn't spend each day at risk of joining the dead. Despite it all, beauty seemed to reign. "As long as this exists," Anne thought to herself, "this sunshine and this cloudless sky, and as long as I can enjoy it, how can I be sad?"

She would later write in her diary that nature was a kind of cure-all, a comfort available to any and all who suffer. Indeed, whether it was the blooming of spring or the starkness of winter, even when it was dark and raining, when it was too dangerous to open the window and she had to sit in the stifling, suffocating heat to do it, Anne always managed to find in nature something to boost her spirits and center herself. "Beauty remains, even in misfortune," she wrote. "If you just look for it, you discover more and more happiness and regain your balance."

How true that is. And what a source of peace and strength it can be.

The trackless woods. A quiet child, lying on her belly, reading a book. The clouds cutting over the wing of an airplane, its exhausted passengers all asleep. A man reading in his seat. A woman sleeping. A stewardess resting her feet. The rosy fingertips of dawn coming up over the mountain. A song on repeat. That song's beat, lining up exactly with the rhythm of events. The pleasure of getting an assignment in before a deadline, the temporary quiet of an empty inbox.

This is stillness.

Rose Lane Wilder wrote of looking out over the grassy plateau in Tbilisi, the capital of Georgia:

> Here there was only sky, and a stillness made audible by the brittle grass. Emptiness was so perfect all around me that I felt a part of it, empty myself; there was a moment in which I was nothing at all—almost nothing at all.

The term for this is *exstasis*—a heavenly experience that lets us step outside ourselves. And these beautiful moments are available to us whenever we want them. All we have to do is open our souls to them.

There is a story about the Zen master Hyakujo, who was approached by two students as he began his morning chores on the farm attached to his temple. When the students asked him to teach them about the Way, he replied, "You open the farm for me and I will talk to you about the great principle of Zen." After they finished their labors and walked to the master for their lesson, he simply turned to face the fields, which the sun was just then rising above, extended his arms out in the direction of the serene expanse, and said nothing.

That was the Way. Nature. The cultivated soil. The growing crops. The satisfaction of good hard work. The poetry of the earth. As it was in the beginning, as it will be forever.

Not that all beauty is so immediately beautiful. We're not always on the farm or at the beach or gazing out over sweeping canyon views. Which is why the philosopher must cultivate the poet's eye—the ability to see beauty everywhere, even in the banal or the terrible.

Marcus Aurelius, who is supposedly this dark, depressive Stoic, loved beauty in his own Whitmanesque way. Why else would he write so vividly of the ordinary way that "baking bread splits in places and those cracks, while not intended in the baker's art, catch our eye and serve to stir our appetite," or the "charm and allure" of nature's process, the "stalks of ripe grain bending low, the frowning brow of the lion, the foam dripping from the boar's mouth." Even of dying, he writes, "Pass through this brief patch of time in harmony with nature. Come to your final resting place gracefully, just as a ripened olive might drop, praising the earth that nourished it and grateful to the tree that gave it growth."

The philosopher and the poet, seeing the world the same way, both engaged in the same pursuit, as Thomas Aquinas said, the study of "wonder."

It was Edward Abbey, the environmental activist and writer, who said that even the word *wildness* itself was music. It's music we can listen to anytime we like, wherever we live, whatever we do for a living. Even if we can't visit, we can think of traipsing through the pine-bedded floor of the forest, of drifting down a slow-moving river, of the warmth of a campfire. Or, like Anne Frank, we can simply look out our window to see a tree. In doing this, in *noticing,* we become alive to the stillness.

It is not the sign of a healthy soul to find beauty in superficial things—the adulation of the crowd, fancy cars, enormous estates, glittering awards. Nor to be made miserable by the ugliness of the world—the critics and haters, the suffering of the innocent, injuries, pain and loss. It is better to find beauty in all places and things. Because it does surround us. And will nourish us if we let it.

The soft paw prints of a cat on the dusty trunk of a car. The hot steam wafting from the vents on a New York City morning. The smell of asphalt just as the rain begins to fall. The thud of a fist fitting perfectly into an open hand. The sound of a pen signing a contract, binding two parties together. The courage of a mosquito sucking blood from a human who can so easily crush it. A basket full of vegetables from the garden. The hard right angles that passing trucks cut out of the drooping branches of trees next to a busy road. A floor filled with a child's toys, arranged in the chaos of exhausted enjoyment. A city arranged the same way, the accumulation of hundreds of years of spasmodic, independent development.

Are you starting to see how this works?

It's ironic that stillness is rare and fleeting in our busy lives, because the world creates an inexhaustible supply of it. It's just that nobody's looking.

After his breakdown and nearly two years of struggle and depression resulting from overstimulation and too much study, where did John Stuart Mill find peace again for the first time? In the poetry of William Wordsworth. And what was the inspiration of so much of Wordsworth's poetry? Nature.

Theodore Roosevelt was sent west by his doctor after the

death of his mother and wife to lose himself in the bigness of the Dakota Badlands. Yes, Teddy was a hunter and a rancher and a man's man, but his two greatest passions? Sitting quietly on a porch with a book and *birdwatching*. The Japanese have a concept, *shinrin yoku*—forest bathing—which is a form of therapy that uses nature as a treatment for mental and spiritual issues. Hardly a week passed, even when he was president, that Roosevelt didn't take a forest bath of some kind.

How much cleaner we would feel if we took these baths as often as we took hot showers. How much more present we would be if we *saw* what was around us.

Bathe is an important word. There is something about water, isn't there? The sight of it. The sound of it. The feel of it. Those seeking stillness could find worse ways to wash away the troubles and turbulence of the world than actual water. A dive into a nearby river. The bubbling fountain in a Zen garden. The reflecting pool of a memorial for those we have lost. Even, in a pinch, a sound machine loaded with the noises of the crashing ocean waves.

To those reeling from trauma or a stressful profession as much as to those suffering from the ennui of modern life, Professor John Stilgoe has simple advice:

> Get out now. Not just outside, but beyond the trap of the programmed electronic age so gently closing around so many people. . . . Go outside, move deliberately, then relax, slow down, look around. Do not jog. Do not run. . . .

Instead pay attention to everything that abuts the rural road, the city street, the suburban boulevard. Walk. Stroll. Saunter. Ride a bike and coast along a lot. Explore.

There is peace in this. It is always available to you.

Don't let the beauty of life escape you. See the world as the temple that it is. Let every experience be churchlike. Marvel at the fact that any of this exists—that *you* exist. Even when we are killing each other in pointless wars, even when we are killing ourselves with pointless work, we can stop and bathe in the beauty that surrounds us, always.

Let it calm you. Let it cleanse you.

ACCEPT A HIGHER POWER

Mediocrity knows nothing higher than itself.

—ARTHUR CONAN DOYLE

For nearly a hundred years, one of the most difficult steps in the twelve steps of "recovery" has not been producing a fearless moral inventory of one's failings or the making of amends. It's not admitting you have a problem, finding a sponsor, or attending meetings.

The step that many addicts—particularly the ones who fancy themselves *thinkers*—struggle with intensely is the acknowledgment of the existence of a *higher power*. They just don't want to admit that they "have come to believe a Power greater than themselves could restore them to sanity."

This seemingly simple step is hard, but not because the world has become increasingly secular since Alcoholics Anonymous's founding in 1935. In fact, one of the founders of AA was, in his words, a "militant agnostic." Acknowledging a higher power is difficult because submitting to anything other than their own desires is anathema to what one addict describes as the "pathological self-centeredness" of addiction.

"I don't believe in God" is the most common objection to Step 2. "There's no evidence of a higher power," they say. "Look at evolution. Look at science." Or they might question what the hell any of this has to do with sobriety anyway. Can't they just stop using drugs and follow the other steps? "What does religion or faith have to do with anything?"

These are perfectly reasonable questions. And yet they don't matter.

Because Step 2 isn't really about God. It's about *surrender*. It's about faith.

Remember, the only way to get over the willful will—the force that Awa Kenzo believed was causing everyone, not just addicts, to miss the targets we aim for—is to let go, at the deep, soul level.

While addiction is undoubtedly a biological disease, it is also, in a more practical sense, a process of becoming obsessed with one's own self and the primacy of one's urges and thoughts. Therefore, admitting that there is something bigger than you out there is an important breakthrough. It means an addict finally understands that they are not God, that they are not in control, and really never have been. By the way, *none* of us are.

The twelve-step process is not itself transformative. It's the decision to stop and to listen and to *follow* that does all the work.

If you really look at the teachings, Alcoholics Anonymous

doesn't say you have to believe in Jesus or go to church. Only that you accept "God as we understand him." That means that if you want to believe in Mother Earth, or Providence, or Destiny, or Fate, or Random Luck, that's up to you.

To the Stoics, their higher power was the *logos*—the path of the universe. They acknowledged fate and fortune and the power these forces had over them. And in acknowledging these higher powers, they accessed a kind of stillness and peace (most simply because it meant less fighting battles for control!) that helped them run empires, survive slavery or exile, and ultimately even face death with great poise. In Chinese philosophy, *dao*—the Way—is the natural order of the universe, the way of a higher spirit. The Greeks not only believed in many different gods, but also that individuals were accompanied by a *daemon,* a guiding spirit that led them to their destiny.

The Confucians believed in Tian, 天—a concept of heaven that guided us while we were here on earth and assigned us a role or purpose in life. The Hindus believed that Brahman was the highest universal reality. In Judaism, Yahweh (יהוה) is the word for Lord. Each of the major Native American tribes had their own word for the Great Spirit, who was their creator and guiding deity. Epicurus wasn't an atheist but rejected the idea of an overbearing or judgmental god. What deity would want the world to live in fear? Living in fear, he said, is incongruent with *ataraxia*.

When Krishna speaks of the "mind resting in the stillness of the prayer of Yoga," it is the same thing. The Christians believe that God is that source of stillness in our lives, which extended peace and comfort to us like a river. "Peace! Be still!" Jesus said to the sea, "and the wind ceased and there was a great calm."

There is no stillness to the mind that thinks of nothing but itself, nor will there ever be peace for the body and spirit that follow their every urge and value nothing but themselves.

The progress of science and technology is essential. But for many of us moderns, it has come at the cost of losing the capacity for awe and for acknowledging forces beyond our comprehension. It has deprived us of the ability to access spiritual stillness and piety.

Are we really to say that a simple peasant who piously believed in God, who worshipped daily in a beautiful cathedral that must have seemed a wondrous glory to the greatness of the Holy Spirit, was worse off than us because he or she lacked our technology or an understanding of evolution? If we told a Zen Buddhist from Japan in the twelfth century that in the future everyone could count on greater wealth and longer lives but that in most cases those gifts would be followed by a feeling of utter purposelessness and dissatisfaction, do you think they would want to trade places with us?

Because that doesn't sound like progress.

In his 1978 commencement address to the students of Harvard, Aleksandr Solzhenitsyn spoke of a modern world where all countries—capitalist and communist alike—had been pervaded by a "despiritualized and irreligious humanistic consciousness."

To such consciousness, man is the touchstone in judging everything on earth—imperfect man, who is never free of pride, self-interest, envy, vanity, and dozens of other defects. We are now experiencing the consequences of mistakes which had not been noticed at the beginning of the journey. On the way from the Renaissance to our days we have enriched our experience, but we have lost the concept of a Supreme Complete Entity which used to restrain our passions and our irresponsibility. We have placed too much hope in political and social reforms, only to find out that we were being deprived of our most precious possession: our spiritual life.

Realism is important. Pragmatism and scientism and skepticism are too. They all have their place. But still, you have to believe in *something*. You just have to. Or else everything is empty and cold.

The comedian Stephen Colbert survived a tragic childhood guided by a deep and earnest Catholic faith that he maintains to this day (teaching Sunday school well into his show business career). His mother, who bore the brunt of that tragedy when she lost her husband and two sons in a plane crash, was his example. "Try to look at this moment in the light of eternity," she would tell him. *Eternity.* Something bigger than us. Something bigger than we can possibly comprehend. Something longer than our tiny humanness naturally considers.

We could find a similar story for just about every faith.

It is probably not a coincidence that when one looks back at history and marvels at the incredible adversity and unimaginable difficulty that people made it through, you tend to find that they all had one thing in common: Some kind of belief in a higher deity. An anchor in their lives called faith. They believed an unfailing hand rested on the wheel, and that there was some deeper purpose or meaning behind their suffering even if they couldn't understand it. It's not a coincidence that the vast majority of people who did good in the world did too.

The reformer Martin Luther was called before a tribunal demanding that he recant his beliefs, on threat of denunciation and possibly death. He spent hours in prayer as he waited his turn to testify. He breathed in. He emptied his mind of worry and fear. He spoke. "I cannot and I will not retract, for it is unsafe for a Christian to speak against his conscience. Here I stand, I can do no other; so help me God. Amen."

Is it not interesting that the leaders who end up truly tested by turbulent times end up sincerely relying on some measure of faith and belief to get them through difficult times?

That was the story of Lincoln. Like many smart young people, he was an atheist early in life, but the trials of adulthood, especially the loss of his son and the horrors of the Civil War, turned him into a believer. Kennedy spent most of his life looking down on his parents' Catholicism . . . but you can bet he was praying as he stood up to the threat of nuclear annihilation.

Here I stand, I can do no other; so help me God.

Nihilism is a fragile strategy. It's always the nihilists who seem to go crazy or kill themselves when life gets hard. (Or, more recently, are so afraid of dying that they obsess about living forever.)

Why is that? Because the nihilist is forced to wrestle with the immense complexity and difficulty and potential emptiness of life (and death) with nothing but their own mind. This is a comically unfair mismatch.

Again, when nearly all the wise people of history agree, we should pause and reflect. It's next to impossible to find an ancient philosophical school that does not talk about a higher power (or higher powers). Not because they had "evidence" of its existence, but because they knew how powerful faith and belief were, how essential they were to the achievement of stillness and inner peace.

Fundamentalism is different. Epicurus was right—if God exists, why would they possibly want you to be afraid of them? And why would they care what clothes you wear or how many times you pay obeisance to them per day? What interest would they have in monuments or in fearful pleas for forgiveness? At the purest level, the only thing that matters to any father or mother— or any creator—is that their children find peace, find meaning, find purpose. They certainly did not put us on this planet so we could judge, control, or kill each other.

But this is not the problem most of us are dealing with. Instead we struggle with skepticism, with an egotism that puts us at the center of the universe. That's why the philosopher Nassim

Taleb's line is so spot on: *It's not that we need to believe that God is great, only that God is greater than us.*

Even if we are the products of evolution and randomness, does this not take us right back to the position of the Stoics? As subjects to the laws of gravity and physics, are we not already accepting a higher, inexplicable power?

We have so little control of the world around us, so many inexplicable events created this world, that it works out almost exactly the same way as if there was a god.

The point of this belief is in some ways to override the mind. To quiet it down by putting it in true perspective. The common language for accepting a higher power is about "letting [Him or Her or It] into your heart." That's it. This is about rejecting the tyranny of our intellect, of our immediate observational experience, and accepting something bigger, something beyond ourselves.

Perhaps you're not ready to do that, to let anything into your heart. That's okay. There's no rush.

Just know that this step is open to you. It's waiting. And it will help restore you to sanity when you're ready.

ENTER RELATIONSHIPS

There is no enjoying the possession of anything
valuable unless one has someone to share it with.

—SENECA

After his first marriage fell apart in the 1960s, the song-
writer Johnny Cash moved from Southern California to
Tennessee. On the first night in his new home, lonely and depressed, he began to pace the length of the ground floor. It was
an enormous house, all but empty of furniture, wedged between
a steep hill on one side and Old Hickory Lake on the other. As he
walked from one end of the floor to the other, from the hill to the
lake, he began to feel, almost frantically, that something was
absent.

What's missing? he thought. *Where is it?* he repeated, over
and over again. Had he forgotten to pack something? Was there
something he needed to do? What wasn't right?

Suddenly, it came to him. It wasn't *something,* it was *someone.*

His young daughter, Rosanne. She wasn't there. She was in California with her mother. A house without family is no home. Johnny Cash stopped, began to shout her name as loud as he could, and fell to the ground and wept.

In some sense, it might seem like that is exactly the kind of anguish that philosophy helps us avoid through the cultivation of detachment and indifference to other people. If you don't make yourself dependent on anyone, if you don't make yourself vulnerable, you can never lose them and you'll never be hurt.

There are people who try to live this way. They take vows of chastity or solitude, or, conversely, try to reduce relationships to their most transactional or minimal form. Or because they have been hurt before, they put up walls. Or because they are so talented, they dedicate themselves exclusively to their work. It is necessary, they say, for they have a higher calling. The Buddha, for instance, walked out on his wife and young son without even saying goodbye, because enlightenment was more important.

Yes, every individual should make the life choices that are right for them. Still, there is something deeply misguided—and terribly sad—about a solitary existence.

It is true that relationships take time. They also expose and distract us, cause pain, and cost money.

We are also nothing without them.

Bad relationships are common, and good relationships are hard. Should that surprise us? Being close to and connecting with other people challenges every facet of our soul.

Especially when our inner child is there, acting out. Or we

are pulled away by lust and desire. Or our selfishness makes little room for another person.

The temptations of the world lead us astray, and our tempers hurt the ones we love.

A good relationship requires us to be virtuous, faithful, present, empathetic, generous, open, and willing to be a part of a larger whole. It requires, in order to create growth, real surrender.

No one would say that's easy.

But rising to this challenge—even attempting to rise to it—transforms us . . . if we let it.

Anyone can be rich or famous. Only you can be *Dad* or *Mom* or *Daughter* or *Son* or *Soul Mate* to the people in your life.

Relationships come in many forms. Mentor. Protégé. Parent. Child. Spouse. Best friend.

And even if, as some have argued, maintaining these relationships reduces a person's material or creative success, might the trade be worth it?

"Who is there who would wish to be surrounded by all the riches in the world and enjoy every abundance in life and yet not love or be loved by anyone?" was Cicero's question some two thousand years ago. It echoes on down to us, still true forever.

Even paragons of stillness struggle with what connection and dependence might mean for their careers. Marina Abramović gave a controversial interview in 2016 where she explained her choice to stay single and not to have children. That would have been a disaster for her art, she said. "One only has limited energy in the body, and I would have had to divide it."

Nonsense.

Nonsense that has been internalized by countless driven and ambitious people.

How well they would do to take even a cursory look at history and literature. German chancellor Angela Merkel has been tirelessly supported by her husband, a man she has described as vital to her success, and upon whose advice she depends. Gertrude Stein was tirelessly supported by her life partner, Alice B. Toklas. Madame Curie was long cynical about love, until she met Pierre, whom she married and with whom she collaborated and ultimately won a Nobel Prize. What about the dedication to *On Liberty*, John Stuart Mill's greatest work, where he calls his wife "inspirer, and in part the author, of all that is best in my writings"? The rapper J. Cole has said that the best thing he ever did as a musician was become a husband and a father. "There was no better decision I could have made," he said, "than the discipline I put on myself of having responsibility, having another human being—my wife—that I have to answer to."

Stillness is best not sought alone. And, like success, it is best when shared. We all need someone who understands us better than we understand ourselves, if only to keep us honest.

Relationships are not a productivity hack, though understanding that love and family are not incompatible with *any* career is a breakthrough. It is also true that the single best decision you can make in life, professionally *and* personally, is to find a partner who complements and supports you and makes you better and for whom you do the same. Conversely, choosing partners and friends who do the opposite endangers both career and happiness.

Life without relationships, focused solely on accomplishment, is empty and meaningless (in addition to being precarious and fragile). A life solely about work and doing is terribly out of balance; indeed, it requires constant motion and busyness to keep from falling apart.

The writer Philip Roth spoke proudly late in life about living alone and being responsible or committed to nothing but his own needs. He once told an interviewer that his lifestyle meant he could be always on call for his work, never having to wait for or on anyone but himself. "I'm like a doctor and it's an emergency room," he said. "And I'm the emergency."

That may be just about the saddest thing a person has ever said without realizing it.

Dorothy Day, the Catholic nun, spoke of the *long loneliness* we all experience, a form of suffering to which the only solution is love and relationships. And yet some people inflict this on themselves on purpose! They deprive themselves of the heaven that is having someone to care about and to care about you in return.

The world hurls at us so many hurricanes. Those who have decided to go through existence as an island are the most exposed and the most ravaged by the storms and whirlwinds.

On September 11, 2001, Brian Sweeney was a passenger trapped on hijacked United Airlines Flight 175, which was heading straight for the South Tower of the World Trade Center. He called his wife from one of the plane's seatback phones to say that things were not looking good. "I want you to know that I absolutely love you," he told her voicemail. "I want you to do good, have good times, same with my parents. I'll see you when you get here."

Imagine the terror of that moment, yet when you hear his voice coming through the phone, not a trace of fear. The same serene calmness is found in the final letter written by Major Sullivan Ballou in 1861 in the days before his Federal regiment marched out to Manassas, Virginia, where he seemed to know for certain that he would die in battle. "Sarah," he wrote, "my love for you is deathless. It seems to bind me with mighty cables, that nothing but Omnipotence can break; and yet, my love of country comes over me like a strong wind, and bears me irresistibly on with all those chains, to the battlefield. The memories of all the blissful moments I have spent with you come crowding over me, and I feel most deeply grateful to God and you, that I have enjoyed them so long."

Fyodor Dostoevsky once described his wife, Anna, as a rock on which he could lean and rest, a wall that would not let him fall and protected him from the cold. There is no better description of love, between spouses or friends or parent and child, than that. Love, Freud said, is the *great educator.* We learn when we give it. We learn when we get it. We get closer to stillness through it.

Like all good education, it is not easy. Not easy at all.

It's been said that the word "love" is spelled T-I-M-E. It is also spelled W-O-R-K and S-A-C-R-I-F-I-C-E and D-I-F-F-I-C-U-L-T-Y, C-O-M-M-I-T-M-E-N-T, and occasionally M-A-D-N-E-S-S.

But it is always punctuated by *R-E-W-A-R-D*. Even ones that end.

The stillness of two people on a porch swing, the stillness of a hug, of a final letter, of a memory, a phone call before a plane crash, of paying it forward, of teaching, of learning, of being *together*.

The notion that isolation, that total self-driven focus, will get you to a supreme state of enlightenment is not only incorrect, it misses the obvious: Who will even care that you did all that? Your house might be quieter without kids and it might be easier to work longer hours without someone waiting for you at the dinner table, but it is a hollow quiet and an empty ease.

To go through our days looking out for no one but ourselves? To think that we can or must do this all alone? To accrue mastery or genius, wealth or power, solely for our own benefit? What is the point?

By ourselves, we are a fraction of what we can be.

By ourselves, something is missing, and, worse, we *feel* that in our bones.

Which is why stillness requires other people; indeed, it is *for* other people.

CONQUER YOUR ANGER

He that is slow to anger is better than the mighty; and
he that ruleth his spirit than he that taketh a city.

—PROVERBS 16:32

In 2009, Michael Jordan was inducted into the Basketball Hall of Fame. It was the crowning achievement of a magnificent career that included six NBA championships, fourteen trips to the All-Star Game, two Olympic gold medals, and the highest scoring average in the history of the sport.

Ascending the stage in a silver suit, with his trademark single hoop earring, Michael was in tears from the start. He joked that his initial plan had been to simply accept the honor, say thank you, and then return to his seat. But he couldn't do it.

He had something he wanted to say.

What ensued was a strange and surreal speech where Michael Jordan, a man with nothing to prove and so much to be thankful for, spent nearly a half hour listing and responding to every slight he'd ever received in his career. Standing at the podium, in a tone that feigned lightheartedness but was clearly deeply felt and deeply angry, he complained of media naysayers, and of how his college coach at North Carolina, Dean Smith, had not touted him as a promising freshman in a 1981 interview with *Sports Illustrated*. He even noted how much he spent on tickets for his children for the ceremony.

After a few sweet remarks about his family, Jordan pointed out a man in the audience named Leroy Smith, the player who had gotten Michael's playing time some thirty-one years earlier. Jordan knew that many people thought that his getting cut in high school was a myth. "Leroy Smith was a guy when I got cut he made the team—on the varsity team—and he's here tonight," Michael explained. "He's still the same six-foot-seven guy—he's not any bigger—probably his game is about the same. But he started the whole process with me, because when he made the team and I didn't, I wanted to prove not just to Leroy Smith, not just to myself, but to the coach that picked Leroy over me, I wanted to make sure you understood—you made a mistake, dude."

It's a remarkable window into Michael's mind, for several reasons. First off, it shows how he had twisted a predictable decision into a major slight about his self-worth. Jordan hadn't been *cut* from any team. He and Leroy had both tried out for a single spot on the varsity team. One had made it. That's not getting "cut"—it's expected that an underclassman won't make the senior class team! Nor had it even been a referendum on his abilities. Leroy was six foot seven. Michael was five foot eleven at the time. It's also so childishly self-absorbed. As if Leroy and his coach weren't their own people, a teammate he could have been happy for, a mentor he could have learned from.

Yet for decades Jordan had chosen to be mad about it.

It's almost palpable how uncomfortable the audience grew as the complaints grew increasingly personal and petty. At one point, Michael mentioned a remark that Jerry Krause made in 1997, supposedly saying that "organizations win championships," not just individual players. Sneering at this minor—but true—observation of the Bulls' general manager, Michael explained that he had specifically not invited Krause to the ceremony in retaliation. He mentioned with pride the time he kicked Pat Riley, the coach of the Lakers, the Knicks, and later the Heat, out of a hotel suite in Hawaii because he wanted to stay in it.

Friends understood that Michael had intended for the speech to be helpful. Instead of uttering a few platitudes, he wanted to show just what it was that created a winning mentality. How tough it was. What it took. He wanted to illustrate how productive anger could be—how as a player each time he was slighted, each time he was underestimated, each time someone didn't do things *his* way, it made him a better player.

The problem is that he delivered almost the exact opposite

message.* Yes, he had shown that anger was powerful fuel. He had also shown just how likely it is to blow up all over yourself and the people around you.

There were undoubtedly moments in Jordan's career when resentment had worked to his advantage and made him play better. It was also a form of madness that hurt him and his teammates (like Steve Kerr and Bill Cartwright and Kwame Brown, whom he physically fought or berated). It had cruelly wrecked the self-confidence of competitors like Muggsy Bogues ("Shoot it, you fucking midget," he'd told his five-foot-three opponent while giving him a free shot in the '95 playoffs). In training camp in 1989, Jordan threw a vicious elbow that knocked a rookie named Matt Brust unconscious, and ended the man's hopes of an NBA career.

Jordan's game was beautiful, but his conduct was often savage and ugly.

Was anger really the secret of Michael Jordan's championships? (Did his anger get him that varsity spot he wanted the next year . . . or did growing four inches help?) Could it have actually been a parasitic by-product that prevented him from enjoying what he accomplished? (Tom Brady wins a lot without being mean or angry.)

If history is any indication, leaders, artists, generals, and

---

*Everyone, that is, but Tiger Woods, who told his golf coach, "I get it. That's what it takes to be as good as MJ. You are always finding ways to get yourself going." It was also Jordan who was partly responsible for introducing Woods to the gambler lifestyle in Las Vegas.

athletes who are driven primarily by anger not only tend to fail over a long enough timeline, but they tend to be miserable even if they don't. It was without a hint of self-awareness that Nixon—who hated Ivy Leaguers, hated reporters, hated Jews and so many other people—said these high-minded words to his loyal staffers in his last hours in the White House: "Always remember, others may hate you, but those who hate you don't win unless you hate them. And then you destroy yourself."

He was right. His own downfall proved it.

The leaders we truly respect, who stand head and shoulders above the rest, have been motivated by more than anger or hate. From Pericles to Martin Luther King Jr., we find that great leaders are fueled by love. Country. Compassion. Destiny. Reconciliation. Mastery. Idealism. Family.

Even in Jordan's case, he was most inspiring not when he was trying to dominate someone but when he was playing for the *love of the game*. And his rings all came under the tutelage and coaching of Phil Jackson, known in basketball as the "Zen Master."

It would be unfair to say that Michael Jordan was as tortured or pained as Richard Nixon, or that he was utterly without joy or happiness. Still, the speech is striking. He had locked so much anger and pain up in a closet in his soul that, at some point, the doors burst open and the mess poured out.

Seneca's argument was that anger ultimately blocks us from whatever goal we are trying to achieve. While it might temporarily help us achieve success in our chosen field, in the long run it is destructive. How excellent is excellence if it doesn't make us feel content, happy, fulfilled? It's a strange bargain that winning, as Jordan illustrated, should require us to constantly think of the times we were made to feel like a loser. The reward for becoming world-class should not be that you are a walking open wound, a trigger that's pulled a thousand times a day.

And what of the people whose anger is more of a hot flash than a slow burn? Seneca once more:

> There is no more stupefying thing than anger, nothing more bent on its own strength. If successful, none more arrogant, if foiled, none more insane—since it's not driven back by weariness even in defeat, when fortune removes its adversary it turns its teeth on itself.

Anger is counterproductive. The flash of rage here, an outburst at the incompetence around us there—this may generate a moment of raw motivation or even a feeling of relief, but we rarely tally up the frustration they cause down the road. Even if we apologize or the good we do outweighs the harm, damage remains—and consequences follow. The person we yelled at is now an enemy. The drawer we broke in a fit is now a constant annoyance. The high blood pressure, the overworked heart, inching us closer to the attack that will put us in the hospital or the grave.

We can pretend we didn't hear or see things that were meant to offend. We can move slowly, giving extreme emotions time to dissipate. We can avoid situations and people (and even entire cities) where we know we tend to get upset or pissed off. When we feel our temper rising up, we need to look for insertion points (the space between stimulus and response). Points where we can get up and walk away. When we can say, "I am getting upset by this and I would like not to lose my cool about it," or "This doesn't matter and I'm not going to hold on to it." We can think even of the Mr. Rogers verse about anger:

> *It's great to be able to stop*
> *When you've planned a thing that's wrong,*
> *And be able to do something else instead*
> *And think this song*

As silly as those lyrics might seem to us in the moment, as our temper is boiling over, are they any worse than a grown adult losing their cool over some minor slight? Are they worse than saying or doing something that will haunt us, possibly forever?

Not that regret minimization is the point of managing our temper, although it is an important factor. The point is that people who are driven by anger are not happy. They are not still. They get in their own way. They shorten legacies and short-circuit their goals.

The Buddhists believed that anger was a kind of tiger within us, one whose claws tear at the body that houses it. To have a chance at stillness—and the clear thinking and big-picture view that defines it—we need to tame that tiger before it kills us. We have to beware of desire, but *conquer* anger, because anger hurts not just ourselves but many other people as well. Although the Stoics are often criticized for their rigid rules and discipline, that is really what they are after: an inner dignity and propriety that protects them and their loved ones from dangerous passions.

Clearly, basketball was a refuge for Michael Jordan, a game he loved and that provided him much satisfaction. But in the pursuit of winning and domination, he also turned it into a kind of raw, open wound, one that seemed to never stop bleeding or cause pain. One that likely cost him additional years of winning, as well as the simple enjoyment of a special evening at the Hall of Fame in Springfield, Massachusetts.

That can't be what you want. That can't be who you want to be.

Which is why we must choose to drive out anger and replace it with love and gratitude—and purpose. Our stillness depends on our ability to slow down and choose *not* to be angry, to run on different fuel. Fuel that helps us win and build, and doesn't hurt other people, our cause, or our chance at peace.

ALL IS ONE

All that you behold, that which comprises both god
and man, is one—we are the parts of one great body.

—SENECA

I n 1971, the astronaut Edgar Mitchell was launched into space.
From 239,000 miles up, he stared down at the tiny blue mar-
ble that is our planet and felt something wash over him. It was,
he said later, "an instant global consciousness, a people orienta-
tion, an intense dissatisfaction with the state of the world, and a
compulsion to do something about it."

So far away, the squabbles of the earth suddenly seemed
petty. The differences between nations and races fell away, the
false urgency of trivial problems disappeared. What was left
was a sense of connectedness and compassion for everyone and
everything.

All Mitchell could think of, when he looked at the planet
from the quiet, weightless cabin of his spaceship, was grabbing

every selfish politician by the neck and pulling them up there to point and say, "Look at that, you son of a bitch."

Not that he was angry. On the contrary, he was the calmest and most serene he'd ever been. He wanted them—the leaders, the people who are supposed to work on behalf of their fellow citizens—to have the same realization he was having: the realization that we are all one, that we are all in this together, and that this fact is the *only* thing that truly matters.

The Christian word for this term is *agape*. It is the ecstasy of love from a higher power, the sheer luck and good fortune of being made in that image. If you've ever seen the Bernini statue of Saint Teresa, you can get a sense of this feeling in the physical form. The caring smile of an angel thrusting an arrow into Teresa's heart. The rays of golden sun shooting down from heaven. Teresa's closed eyes and partly opened mouth, realizing, *knowing* the depth of love and connection that exists for her.

Whether it comes from the perspective of space, a religious epiphany, or the silence of meditation, the understanding that we are all connected—*that we are all one*—is a transformative experience.

Such quiet peace follows this . . . such stillness.

With it, we lose the selfishness and self-absorption at the root of much of the disturbance in our lives.

The Greeks spoke of *sympatheia,* the kind of mutual interdependence and relatedness of all things, past, present, and future. They believed that each person on this planet had an important role to play, and should be respected for it. John Cage came to understand something similar as he embraced his own quirky, unique style of music—like that four-minute-and-thirty-three-second song of silence—rather than trying to be like everyone else. "That one sees that the human race as one person," he wrote, with each of us as an individual part of one single body, "enables him to see that originality is necessary, for there is no need for eye to do what hand does so well."

The truly philosophical view is that not only is originality necessary, but *everyone* is necessary. Even the people you don't like. Even the ones who really piss you off. Even the people wasting their lives, cheating, or breaking the rules are part of the larger equation. We can appreciate—or at least sympathize with—them, rather than try to fight or change them.

Robert Greene, known for his amoral study of power and seduction, actually writes in his book *The Laws of Human Nature* about the need to practice *mitfreude,* the active wishing of goodwill to other people, instead of *schadenfreude,* the active wishing of ill will. We can make an active effort to practice forgiveness, especially to those who might have caused those inner-child wounds we have worked to heal. We can seek understanding with those we disagree with. *Tout comprendre c'est tout pardonner.* To understand all is to forgive all. To love all is to be at peace with all, including yourself.

Take something you care about deeply, a possession you cherish, a person you love, or an experience that means a lot to you. Now take that feeling, that radiating warmth that comes up when you think about it, and consider how *every single person,* even murderers on death row, even the jerk who just shoved you in the supermarket, has that same feeling about something in their lives. Together, you share that. Not only do you share it, but you share it with everyone who has ever lived. It connects you to Cleopatra and Napoleon and Frederick Douglass.

You can do the same with your pain. As bad as you might feel in a given moment, this too is a shared feeling, a connection with others. The man stepping outside to take a walk after an argument with his spouse. The mother worrying about her child, the one who seems to always be in trouble. The merchant stressing over where the money will come from—*How will I keep going?* Two siblings grieving the loss of a parent. The average citizen following the news, hoping their country will avoid an unnecessary war.

No one is alone, in suffering or in joy. Down the street, across the ocean, in another language, someone else is experiencing nearly the exact same thing. It has always been and always will be thus.

You can even use this to connect more deeply with yourself and your own life. The moon you're looking at tonight is the same moon you looked at as a scared young boy or girl, it's the same you'll look at when you're older—in moments of joy and in pain—and it's the same that your children will look at in their own moments and their own lives.

When you step back from the enormity of your own immediate experience—whatever it is—you are able to see the experience of others and either connect with them or lessen the intensity of your own pain. We are all strands in a long rope that stretches back countless generations and ties together every person in every country on every continent. We are all thinking and feeling the same things, we are all made of and motivated by the same things. We are all stardust. And no one needs this understanding more than the ambitious or the creative, since they live so much in their own heads and in their own bubble.

Finding the universal in the personal, and the personal in the universal, is not only the secret to art and leadership and even entrepreneurship, it is the secret to centering oneself. It both turns down the volume of noise in the world and tunes one in to the quiet wavelength of wisdom that sages and philosophers have long been on.

This connectedness and universality does not need to stop at our fellow man. The philosopher Martha Nussbaum recently pointed out the narcissism of the human obsession with what it means to be human. A better, more open, more vulnerable, more connected question is to ask what it means to be alive, or to exist, *period.* As she wrote:

> We share a planet with billions of other sentient be-
> ings, and they all have their own complex ways of being
> whatever they are. All of our fellow animal creatures, as
> Aristotle observed long ago, try to stay alive and repro-
> duce more of their kind. All of them perceive. All of them

desire. And most move from place to place to get what they want and need.

We share much of our DNA with these creatures, we breathe the same air, we walk on the same land and swim in the same oceans. We are inextricably intertwined with each other—as are our fates.

The less we are convinced of our exceptionalism, the greater ability we have to understand and contribute to our environment, the less blindly driven we are by our own needs, the more clearly we can appreciate the needs of those around us, the more we can appreciate the larger ecosystem of which we are a part.

Peace is when we realize that victory and defeat are almost identical spots on one long spectrum. Peace is what allows us to take joy in the success of others and to let them take joy in our own. Peace is what motivates a person to be good, to treat every other living thing well, because they understand that it is a way to treat themselves well.

We are one big collective organism engaged in one endless project together. We are one.

We are the same.

Still, too often we forget it, and we forget ourselves in the process.

ON TO WHAT'S NEXT . . .

> Very few go astray who comport themselves with
> restraint.
>
> —CONFUCIUS

L *'essentiel est invisible pour les yeux.*
What's essential is invisible to the eye.

The quote that hung on Fred Rogers's wall was actually only a partial quote. The rest appears in *The Little Prince,* the beautiful and surreal children's book by the French aviator and World War II hero Antoine de Saint-Exupéry. In it, the fox tells the little boy, "Here is my secret. It is very simple: It is only with the heart that one can see rightly, what is essential is invisible to the eye."

First, we sought mental clarity. But quickly we realized that the soul must be in equally good order if we wish to achieve stillness. In concert with each other—clarity in the mind and in the soul—we find both excellence and unbreakable tranquility. It is with the *heart* and soul that we are able to surface important things that the eyes need to see.

Examining our souls is not as easy as clearing our minds, you'll find. It requires that we peel back what the writer Mark Manson has called the "self-awareness onion" and take responsibility for our own emotions and impulses. Anyone who's done it can tell you that tears and onions often go together.

But it's precisely this soft stuff—getting in touch with ourselves, finding balance and meaning, cultivating virtue—that the volleyball champion Kerri Walsh Jennings has said makes her such a killer on the court.

Some ancient traditions have held that the soul is in the belly, which is fitting for two reasons. Because we've just been through the *belly of the beast* part of our journey, and because it sets up where we go next.

Stillness isn't merely an abstraction—something we only think about or feel. It's also real. It's *in our bodies*. Seneca warned us not to "suppose that the soul is at peace when the body is still." Vice versa. Lao Tzu said that "movement is the foundation of stillness."

What follows then is the final domain of stillness. The literal form that *our form* takes in the course of day-to-day life. Our bodies (where, you must not forget, the heart and the brain are both located). The environment we put those bodies in. The habits and routines to which we subject that body.

A body that is overworked or abused is not only actually not still, it creates turbulence that ripples through the rest of our lives. A mind that is overtaxed and ill-treated is susceptible to vice and corruption. A spoiled, lazy existence is the manifestation of spiritual emptiness. We can be active, we can be on the move, and still be still. Indeed, we have to be active for the stillness to have any meaning.

Life is hard. Fortune is fickle. We can't afford to be weak. We can't afford to be fragile. We must strengthen our bodies as the physical vessel for our minds and spirit, subject to the capriciousness of the physical world.

Which is why we now move on to this final domain of stillness—the body—and its place in the real world. In real life.

PART III

MIND ✦ SPIRIT ✦ **BODY**

We are all sculptors and painters, and our material is
our own flesh and blood and bones.

—HENRY DAVID THOREAU

THE DOMAIN OF THE BODY

Winston Churchill had a productive life.

He first saw combat at age twenty-one, and wrote his first bestselling book about it not long after. By twenty-six, he'd been elected to public office and would serve in government for the next six and half decades. He'd write some ten million words and over forty books, paint more than five hundred paintings, and give some twenty-three hundred speeches in the course of his time on this planet. In between all that, he managed to hold the positions of minister of defense, first lord of the admiralty, chancellor of the exchequer, and of course, prime minister of Britain, where he helped save the world from the Nazi menace. Then, to top it off, he spent his twilight years fighting the totalitarian communist menace.

"It is a pushing age," Churchill wrote his mother as a young man, "and we must shove with the rest." It may well be that Winston Churchill was the greatest pusher in all of history. His life spanned the final cavalry charge of the British Empire, which he witnessed as a young war correspondent in 1898, and ended well into the nuclear age, indeed the space age, both of which he helped usher in. His first trip to America was on a steamship (to be introduced on stage by Mark Twain, no less), and his final one on a Boeing 707 that flew at 500 miles per hour. In between he saw two world wars, the invention of the car, radio, and rock and roll, and countless trials and triumphs.

Is there stillness to be found here? Could someone that active, so Herculean in their labors, who embraced so much strife and stress, ever be described as still, or at peace?

Strangely, yes.

As Paul Johnson, one of Churchill's best biographers, would write, "The balance he maintained between flat-out work and creative and restorative leisure is worth study by anyone holding a top position." Johnson as a seventeen-year-old, decades before his own career as a writer, met Churchill on the street and shouted to him, "Sir, to what do you attribute your success in life?"

Immediately, Churchill replied, "Conservation of energy. Never stand up when you can sit down, and never sit down when you can lie down."

Churchill conserved his energy so that he never shirked from a task, or backed down from a challenge. So that, for all this work and pushing, he never burned himself out or snuffed out the spark of joy that made life worth living. (Indeed, in addition to the importance of hard work, Johnson said the other four lessons from Churchill's remarkable life were to aim high; to never allow mistakes or criticism to get you down; to waste no energy

on grudges, duplicity, or infighting; and to make room for joy.)
Even during the war, Churchill never lost his sense of humor,
never lost sight of what was beautiful in the world, and never became jaded or cynical.

Different traditions offer different prescriptions for the good
life. The Stoics urged determination and iron self-will. The Epicureans preached relaxation and simple pleasures. The Christians spoke of saving mankind and glorifying God. The French,
a certain *joie de vivre*. The happiest and most resilient of us
manage to incorporate a little of each of these approaches into
our lives, and that was certainly true of Churchill. He was a
man of great discipline and passion. He was a soldier. He was
a lover of books, a believer in glory and honor. A statesman, a
literal bricklayer, and a painter. We are all worms, he once joked
to a friend, simple organisms that eat and defecate and then die,
but he liked to think of himself as a *glowworm*.

In addition to his impressive mental abilities and spiritual
strength, Churchill was also an unexpected—given his portly
frame—master of the third and final domain of stillness, the
physical one.

Few would have predicted he would distinguish himself here.
Born with a frail constitution, Churchill complained as a young
man that he was "cursed with so feeble a body that I can hardly
support the fatigues of the day." Yet like Theodore Roosevelt before him, he cultivated inside this frail body an indomitable soul
and a determined mind that overcame his physical limitations.

It's a balance that everyone aspiring to sustained inner peace must strike. *Mens sana in corpore sano*—a strong mind in a strong body. Remember, when we say that someone "showed so much heart," we don't mean emotion. We mean they had tenacity and grit. The metaphor is actually misleading if you think about it. It's really the *spine*—the backbone of body—that's doing the work.

Young Churchill loved the written word, but, diverging from the traditional path of a writer, he didn't lock himself up with books in a dusty old library. He put his body into action. Serving in or observing three straight wars, he made his name chronicling the exploits of the empire, first as a war correspondent in South Africa during the Boer War, where he was taken prisoner in 1899 and barely escaped with his life.

In 1900, he was elected to his first political office. By age thirty-three, realizing that greatness was impossible alone, he committed his body to another. He married his wife, Clementine, a brilliant, calming influence who balanced out many of his worst traits. It was one of the great marriages of the age—they called each other "Pug" and "Cat"—marked by true affection and love. "My ability to persuade my wife to marry me," he said, was "quite my most brilliant achievement. . . . Of course, it would have been impossible for any ordinary man to have got through what I had to go through in peace and war without the devoted aid of what we call, in England, one's better half."

As busy and ambitious as Churchill was—as much of a pusher as he was—he was rarely frantic and did not tolerate disorganization. It almost ruins the fun to learn that Churchill's infamous bons mots and one-liners were in fact well-practiced and re-hearsed. No one knew the effort that went into them, he said, nor the effort that went into making them look effortless. "Every night," he said, "I try myself by court martial to see if I have done anything effective during the day. I don't mean just pawing the ground—anyone can go through the motions—but something really effective."

As a writer, he was gaspingly productive. While holding political office, Churchill managed to publish seven books between 1898 and the end of World War I alone. How did he do it? How did he manage to pull so much out of himself? The simple answer: physical routine.

Each morning, Churchill got up around eight and took his first bath, which he entered at 98 degrees and had cranked up to 104 while he sat (and occasionally somersaulted) in the water. Freshly bathed, he would spend the next two hours reading. Then he responded to his daily mail, mostly pertaining to his political duties. Around noon he'd stop in to say hello to his wife for the first time—believing all his life that the secret to a happy marriage was that spouses should not see each other before noon. Then he tackled whatever writing project he was working on—likely an article or a speech or a book. By early afternoon he would be writing at a fantastic clip and then abruptly stop for lunch (which he would finally dress for). After lunch, he would go for a walk around Chartwell, his estate in the English countryside, feeding his swans and fish—to him the most important and enjoyable part of the day. Then he would sit on the porch and take in the air, thinking and musing. For inspiration and serenity he might recite poetry to himself. At 3 p.m., it was time for a two-hour nap. After the nap, it was family time and then a second bath before a late, seated and formal dinner (after 8 p.m.). After dinner and drinks, one more writing sprint before bed.

It was a routine he would stick to even on Christmas.

Churchill was a hard worker and a man of discipline—but like us, he was not perfect. He often worked more than he should have, usually because he spent more money than he needed to (and it produced a fair bit of writing that would have better remained unpublished). Churchill was impetuous, liked to gamble, and was prone to overcommit. It wasn't from the tireless execution of his wartime duties that he was inspired to depict himself once, in a drawing, as a pig carrying a twenty-thousand-pound weight. It was his indulgences that produced that.

Nor was his life an endless series of triumphs. Churchill made many mistakes, usually lapses of judgment that came from a mind fried by stress. Thus, he emerged from World War I with a mixed record. His service in the wartime administration had been marked by some major failures, but he had redeemed himself by resigning and serving on the front lines with the Royal Scots Fusiliers. After the war, he was called back to serve as secretary of state for war and air and then secretary of state for the colonies.

The mid-1920s saw Churchill serving as chancellor of the exchequer (a position in which he was in way over his head), while having also signed a contract to produce a six-volume, three-thousand-page account of the war, titled *The World Crisis*. Left to his own devices, he might have tried to white-knuckle this incredible workload. But those around him saw the toll that his responsibilities were taking and, worried about burnout, urged him to find a hobby that might offer him a modicum of pleasure and enjoyment and rest. "Do remember what I said about resting from current problems," Prime Minister Stanley Baldwin wrote to him. "A big year will soon begin and much depends on your keeping fit."

In typical Churchillian fashion, he chose an unexpected form of leisure: bricklaying. Taught the craft by two employees at Chartwell, he immediately fell in love with the slow, methodical process of mixing mortar, troweling, and stacking bricks. Unlike his other professions, writing and politics, bricklaying didn't wear down his body, it invigorated him. Churchill could lay as many as ninety bricks an hour. As he wrote to the prime minister in 1927, "I have had a delightful month building a cottage and dictating a book: 200 bricks and 2000 words a day." (He also spent several hours a day on his ministerial duties.) A friend observed how good it was for Churchill to get down on the ground and interact with the earth. This was also precious time he spent with his youngest daughter, Sarah, who dutifully carried the bricks for her father as his cute and well-loved apprentice.

A dark moment in World War I had inspired another hobby— oil painting. He was introduced to it by his sister-in-law, who, sensing that Churchill was a steaming kettle of stress, handed him a small kit of paints and brushes her young children liked to play with. In a little book titled *Painting as a Pastime,* Churchill spoke eloquently of a reliance on new activities that use other parts of our minds and bodies to relieve the areas where we are overworked. "The cultivation of a hobby and new forms of interest is therefore a policy of first importance to a public man," he wrote. "To be really happy and really safe, one ought to have at least two or three hobbies, and they must all be real."

Churchill was not a particularly good painter (his bricklaying was often corrected by professionals too), but even a glance at his pictures reveals how much he enjoyed himself as he worked. It's palpable in the brushstrokes. "Just to paint is great fun," he would say. "The colors are lovely to look at and delicious to squeeze out." Early on, Churchill was advised by a well-known painter never to hesitate in front of the canvas (that is to say, *overthink*), and he took it to heart. He wasn't intimidated or discouraged by his lack of skill (only this could explain the audacity it took for him to add a mouse to a priceless Peter Paul Rubens painting that hung in one of the prime minister's residences). Painting was about expression of joy for Churchill. It was *leisure,* not work.

Painting, like all good hobbies, taught the practitioner to be present. "This heightened sense of observation of Nature," he wrote, "is one of the chief delights that have come to me through trying to paint." He had lived for forty years on planet Earth consumed by his work and his ambition, but through painting, his perspective and perception grew much sharper. Forced to slow down to set up his easel, to mix his paints, to wait for them to dry, he *saw* things he would have previously blown right past.

This was a skill that he actively cultivated—increasing his mental awareness by way of physical exercises. Churchill started going to museums to look at paintings, then he'd wait a day and try to re-create them from memory. Or he'd try to capture a landscape he had seen after he had left it. (This was similar to his habit of reciting poetry aloud.) "Painting challenged his intellect, appealed to his sense of beauty and proportion, unleashed his creative impulse, and . . . brought him peace," remarked his lifelong friend Violet Bonham Carter. It was also, she said, the only thing Churchill ever did silently. His other daughter, Mary, observed that painting and manual labor "were the sovereign antidotes to the depressive element in his nature." Churchill was happy because he got out of his own head and put his body to work.

How necessary this turned out to be, because in 1929 his stunning political career suddenly came to what appeared to be an ignominious end. Driven from political life, Churchill spent a decade in pseudo-exile at Chartwell, while Neville Chamberlain and a generation of British politicians appeased the growing threat of Fascism in Europe.

Life does that to us. It kicks our ass. Everything we work for can be taken away. All our powers can be rendered impotent in a moment. What follows this is not just an issue of spirit or the mind, it's a real physical question: *What do you do with your time? How do you handle the stress of the whiplash?*

Marcus Aurelius's answer was that in these situations one must "love the discipline you know and let it support you." In 1915, reeling from the failure of the Gallipoli campaign, Churchill wrote of feeling like a "sea-beast fished up from the depths, or a diver too suddenly hoisted, my veins threatened to burst from the fall in pressure. I had great anxiety and no means of relieving it; I had vehement convictions and small power to give effect to them." It was then that he picked up painting, and in 1929, experiencing a similar loss in cabin pressure, he returned to his discipline and his hobbies for relief and for reflection.

Churchill didn't know it in the middle of the 1930s, but being out of power during Germany's rearmament was exactly the right place to be. It would take real strength to stay there, to not fight his way back in, but if he had, he would have been sullied by the incompetence of his peers in the government. Churchill was likely one of the only British leaders to take the time to sit through and digest Hitler's *Mein Kampf* (if Chamberlain had, perhaps Hitler could have been stopped sooner). This time allowed Churchill to actively pursue his writing and radio careers, which made him a beloved celebrity in America (and primed the country for its eventual alliance with Britain). He spent time with his goldfish and his children and his oils.

Also, he had to wait. For the first time in his life, excepting those afternoons on the porch, he had to do *nothing*.

Would Churchill have been the outsider called back to lead Britain in its finest hour had he allowed the indignity of his political exile to overwhelm his mind, burrow into his soul, and compel him to fight his way back into the limelight in those years? Could he have had the energy and strength at age sixty-six to put the country on his back and *lead* without that supposedly "lost" decade? If he had kept up his breakneck pace?

Almost certainly not.

Churchill himself would write that every prophet must be forced into the wilderness—where they undergo solitude, deprivation, reflection, and meditation. It's from this physical ordeal he said that "psychic dynamite" is made. When Churchill was recalled, he was ready. He was rested. He could see what no one else could or would. Everyone else cowered in fear of Hitler, but Churchill did not.

Instead, he fought. He stood alone. As he said to the House of Commons:

> Even though large tracts of Europe and many old and famous States have fallen or may fall into the grip of the Gestapo and all the odious apparatus of Nazi rule, we shall not flag or fail. We shall go on to the end, we shall fight in France, we shall fight on the seas and oceans, we shall fight with growing confidence and growing strength in the air, we shall defend our Island, whatever the cost may be, we shall fight on the beaches, we shall fight on the landing grounds, we shall fight in the fields and in the

streets, we shall fight in the hills; we shall never surrender, and even if, which I do not for a moment believe, this
Island or a large part of it were subjugated and starving,
then our Empire beyond the seas, armed and guarded by
the British Fleet, would carry on the struggle, until, in
God's good time, the New World, with all its power and
might, steps forth to the rescue and the liberation of
the old.

Churchill demanded equal courage from those in his own
house. When asked by his daughter-in-law what they could possibly do if the Germans invaded Britain, he growled and replied,
"You can always get a carving knife from the kitchen and take
one with you, can't you?"

The British Empire had been responsible for despicable
human rights violations, but Churchill knew irredeemable evil
when he saw it, and its name was Nazism. Concentration camps
and genocidal extermination still lay off in the future, but
Churchill saw that no self-respecting leader, no country of virtue could make a deal with Hitler. Even if that was easier. Even
if it might have protected Britain from invasion. At the same
time, he was careful to manage the passions that war stirs up. "I
hate nobody except Hitler," he said "and that is professional."

Churchill was an indefatigable workhorse from the day Britain declared war on Germany in 1939 until the end of the war in
mid-1945. During the war, Clementine designed a special suit
her husband could wear *and* sleep in. They were called his "siren

suits"—though the British public endearingly referred to them as his "rompers"—and they saved him precious minutes getting dressed, allowing him to grab much-needed naps.

So, yes, he was out of balance in those years, working 110-hour weeks, and hardly ever still. It has been estimated that he traveled 110,000 miles by air and sea and car between 1940 and 1943 alone. During the war, it was said that Churchill kept "less schedule than a forest fire and had less peace than a hurricane." But then again, he'd rested up for precisely this moment—and when it was an option, he did maintain his routine, even when he was living like a gopher in the underground bunker that was the Cabinet War Rooms. He didn't have much time for painting during the war—nor many chances to be out in nature—but when he could he did. (One is a beautiful painting of a North African sunset, which he drove an extra five hours to capture after the major war powers met at Casablanca.)

It is unlikely that any single individual has ever done more to save or advance the notions sacred to Eastern or Western civilization. And how was Churchill rewarded for these labors, for all that he had done?

In 1945, he was pushed out of office. Upon hearing the news, Clementine attempted to console him by saying, "Perhaps this is a blessing in disguise." "It must be very well-disguised," Churchill replied. He was wrong. She was right. As usual.

Not only because it allowed Churchill to write his final set of memoirs, *The Second World War,* which firmly established and taught the lessons that have prevented the world from veering toward suicide since, but because it allowed him once again to rest up and balance himself. We can see photos of him painting in Marrakech in 1948, in the south of France in the 1950s. In all he would paint some 550 paintings in his lifetime, 145 of them after the war.

It was, in the end, a life of much struggle and sacrifice, a lot of it thankless and misunderstood. It was productive, but at a high personal cost. The same tasks and responsibilities would have burned out and burned through a dozen normal people.

"Was it worth it?" a wearied hero had asked in Churchill's only novel. "The struggle, the labor, the constant rush of affairs, the sacrifice of so many things that make life easy, or pleasant— for what?" He wrote that when he was young, when he had been busy and ambitious, and but not yet truly engaged in public service. In the future lay fifty-five years in Parliament, thirty-one years as a minister, and nine years as prime minister. The years ahead would show him the true meaning of life and what it meant to really fight for causes that mattered. He experienced both triumph and disaster. And by the end of his life, he came to know that it was all worth it—and certainly all of us alive today are grateful for those labors.

Indeed, Churchill's last words were confirmation of this fact:

The journey has been enjoyable and well worth making— once!

Epicurus once said that the wise will accomplish three

things in their life: leave written works behind them, be financially prudent and provide for the future, and cherish country living. That is to say, we will be reflective, we will be responsible and moderate, and we will find time to relax in nature. It cannot be said that Churchill did not do these things well (even granting that he did live it up when he could afford to).

We compare this description to the three words Aristotle used to describe the lives of slaves in his time: "Work, punishment, and food."

Which of these are we closer to in the modern world? Which of these is the path to happiness and stillness?

No one can afford to neglect the final domain in our journey to stillness. What we do with our bodies. What we put *in* our bodies. Where we dwell. What kind of routine and schedule we keep. How we find leisure and relief from the pressures of life.

If we are to be half as productive as Churchill, and manage to capture the same joy and zest and stillness that defined his life, there are traits we will need to cultivate. Each of us will need to:

- Rise above our physical limitations.
- Find hobbies that rest and replenish us.
- Develop a reliable, disciplined routine.
- Spend time getting active outdoors.
- Seek out solitude and perspective.
- Learn to sit—to do nothing when called for.
- Get enough sleep and rein in our workaholism.
- Commit to causes bigger than ourselves.

As they say, the body keeps score. If we don't take care of ourselves physically, if we don't align ourselves properly, it doesn't matter how strong we are mentally or spiritually.

This will take effort. Because we will not simply *think* our way to peace. We can't pray our soul into better condition. We've got to move and live our way there. It will take our body—our habits, our actions, our rituals, our self-care—to get our mind and our spirit in the right place, just as it takes our mind and spirit to get our body to the right place.

It's a trinity. A holy one. Each part dependent on the others.

SAY NO

The advantages of nonaction.
Few in the world attain these.

—*THE DAODEJING*

When Fabius was dispatched to lead the Roman legions against Hannibal, he did nothing. He did not attack. He did not race out to drive the terrifying invader out of Italy and back to Africa.

You might think this was a sign of weakness—certainly most of Rome did—but in fact, it was all part of Fabius's strategy. Hannibal was far from home, he was losing men to the elements and could not easily replace them. Fabius believed that if Rome just held out and did not engage in any costly battles, they would win.

But the mob couldn't handle that kind of deliberate restraint. *We're the strongest army in the world,* his critics said. *We don't sit around doing nothing when someone tries to attack us!* So while Fabius was away attending a religious ceremony, they pressured his commander Minucius to attack.

It did not go well. He ran straight into a trap. Fabius had to rush to his rescue. And even then, Minucius was hailed as a hero for *doing something,* while Fabius was labeled a coward for holding himself back. When his term ended, the Roman assemblies voted to abandon what is now known as a "Fabian strategy" of mostly avoiding battle and wearing Hannibal down, in favor of greater aggression and more action.

It didn't work. Only after the bloodbath at the Battle of Cannae, in which the Romans attacked Hannibal and lost nearly their entire army in a horrific rout, did people finally begin to understand Fabius's wisdom. Now they could see that what had looked like an excess of caution was in fact a brilliant method of warfare. He had been buying time and giving his opponent a chance to destroy himself. Only now—and not a moment too soon—were they ready to listen to him.

While most great Romans were given honorific titles that highlighted their great victories or accomplishments in foreign lands, Fabius was later given one that stands out: *Fabius Cunctator.*

The Delayer.

He was special for what he didn't do—for what he *waited* to do—and has stood as an important example to all leaders since. Especially the ones feeling pressure from themselves or their followers to be bold or take immediate action.

In baseball, you make a name for yourself by swinging for the fences. Particularly for players from small, poor countries, showing your power as a home run hitter is how you get noticed by scouts and coaches. As they say in the Dominican Republic, "You don't walk off the island." Meaning, you *hit* your way off.

It's like life. You can't benefit from opportunities you don't try to take advantage of.

But Dr. Jonathan Fader, an elite sports psychologist who has spent nearly a decade with the New York Mets, has talked about just how problematic this lesson is for rookie players in the majors. They built their reputations, and therefore their identities, on swinging at every pitch they thought they could hit . . . and now they're facing the best pitchers in the world. Suddenly, aggression is a weakness, not a strength. Now they have to get up there in front of millions of people, getting paid millions of dollars, and mostly *not* swing the bat. They have to wait for the perfect pitch.

What they have to learn, what the great hitter Sadaharu Oh himself learned in a series of complicated batting exercises designed by his Zen master and hitting coach, Hiroshi Arakawa, was the power of waiting, the power of precision, the power of the void. Because that's what makes for a real pro. A truly great hitter—not just a *swinger*—needs quick hands and powerful hips, to be sure, but they must also possess the power of *wu wei,* or nonaction.

Wu wei is the ability to hold the bat back—waiting until the batter sees the perfect pitch. It is the yogi in meditation. They're *physically* still, so that they can be active on a mental and spiritual level. That was also Kennedy during the Cuban Missile Crisis. It might have seemed like he wasn't doing enough—that he wasn't rushing to destroy his opponent—but he was rightly carving out the space and time to think, and time and space for the Russians to do the same thing. Practicing *wu wei* was precisely what Tiger Woods lost the ability to do as his work and sex addictions took control.

A *disciplined action,* that's what John Cage called doing nothing in the performance instructions on 4'33".

You don't solve a maze by rushing through. You have to stop and think. You have to walk slowly and carefully, reining in your energy—otherwise you'll get hopelessly lost. The same is true for the problems we face in life.

The green light is a powerful symbol in our culture. We forget what Mr. Rogers was trying to make us see—that the yellow light and the red light are just as important. Slow down. *Stop.* One recent study found that subjects would rather give themselves an electric shock than experience boredom for even a few minutes. Then we wonder why people do so many stupid things.

There is a haunting clip of Joan Rivers, well into her seventies, already one of the most accomplished and respected and talented comedians of all time, in which she is asked why she keeps working, why she is always on the road, always looking for more gigs. Telling the interviewer about the fear that drives her, she holds up an empty calendar. "If my book ever looked like this, it would mean that nobody wants me, that everything I ever tried to do in life didn't work. Nobody cared and I've been totally forgotten."

It's not just that there was never enough for Joan. It's that our best and most lasting work comes from when we take things slow. When we pick our shots and wait for the right pitches.

Somebody who thinks they're nothing and don't matter because they're not doing something for *even a few days* is depriving themselves of stillness, yes—but they are also closing themselves off from a higher plane of performance that comes out of it.

Spiritually, that's hard. Physically, it's harder still. You have to make yourself say no. You have to make yourself *not* take the stage.

A weaker Fabius would not have been able to resist attacking Hannibal, and all of history might have turned out differently. A long-distance runner who can't pace himself. A money manager who can't wait out a bear market. If they can't learn the art of *wu wei* in their professions, they won't succeed. If you can't do it in *your life,* forget about success, you'll burn out your body. And you don't get another one of those!

We should look fearfully, even sympathetically, at the people who have become slaves to their calendars, who require a staff of ten to handle all their ongoing projects, whose lives seem to resemble a fugitive fleeing one scene for the next. There is no stillness there. It's servitude.

Each of us needs to get better at saying no. As in, "No, sorry,

I'm not available." "No, sorry, that sounds great but I'd rather not." "No, I'm going to wait and see." "No, I don't like that idea." "No, I don't need that—I'm going to make the most of what I have." "No, because if I said yes to you, I'd have to say yes to everyone."

Maybe it's not the most virtuous thing to say "No, sorry, I can't" when you really can but just don't want to. But can you really? Can you really afford to do it? And does it not harm other people if you're constantly stretched too thin?

A pilot gets to say, "Sorry, I'm on standby," as an excuse to get out of things. Doctors and firemen and police officers get to use being "on call" as a shield. But are we not on call in our own lives? Isn't there something (or someone) that we're preserving our full capacities for? Are our own bodies not on call for our families, for our self-improvement, for our own work?

Always think about what you're really being asked to give. Because the answer is often *a piece of your life,* usually in exchange for something you don't even want. Remember, that's what time is. It's your life, it's your flesh and blood, that you can never get back.

In every situation ask:

What is it?
Why does it matter?
Do I need it?
Do I want it?
What are the hidden costs?

Will I look back from the distant future and be glad I did it?
If I never knew about it at all—if the request was lost in the
    mail, if they hadn't been able to pin me down to ask me—
    would I even notice that I missed out?

When we know what to say no to, we can say yes to the things
that matter.

TAKE A WALK

It is only ideas gained from walking that have any
worth.

—FRIEDRICH NIETZSCHE

Nearly every afternoon the citizens of Copenhagen were
treated to the strange sight of Søren Kierkegaard walking
the streets. The cantankerous philosopher would write in the
morning at a standing desk, and then around noon would head
out onto the busy streets of the city.

He walked on the newfangled "sidewalks" that had been
built for fashionable citizens to stroll along. He walked through
the city's parks and along the pathways of Assistens Ceme-
tery, where he would later be buried. On occasion, he walked out
past the city's walls and into the countryside. Kierkegaard never
seemed to walk straight—he zigged and zagged, crossing the
street without notice, trying to always remain in the shade.
When he had either worn himself out, worked through what he

was struggling with, or been struck with a good idea, he would turn around and make for home, where he would write for the rest of the day.

Seeing Kierkegaard out walking surprised the residents of Copenhagen, because he seemed, at least from his writings, to be such a high-strung individual. They weren't wrong. Walking was how he released the stress and frustration that his philosophical explorations inevitably created.

In a beautiful letter to his sister-in-law, who was often bedridden, and depressed as a result, Kierkegaard wrote of the importance of walking. "Above all," he told her in 1847, "do not lose your desire to walk: Every day I walk myself into a state of wellbeing and walk away from every illness; I have walked myself into my best thoughts, and I know of no thought so burdensome that one cannot walk away from it."

Kierkegaard believed that sitting still was a kind of breeding ground for illness. But walking, *movement,* to him was almost sacred. It cleansed the soul and cleared the mind in a way that primed his explorations as a philosopher. Life is a path, he liked to say, we have to walk it.

And while Kierkegaard was particularly eloquent in his writing about walking, he was by no means alone in his dedication to the practice—nor alone in reaping the benefits. Nietzsche said that the ideas in *Thus Spoke Zarathustra* came to him on a long walk. Nikola Tesla discovered the rotating magnetic field, one of the most important scientific discoveries of all time, on a walk through a city park in Budapest in 1882. When he lived in

Paris, Ernest Hemingway would take long walks along the quais whenever he was stuck in his writing and needed to clarify his thinking. Charles Darwin's daily schedule included several walks, as did those of Steve Jobs and the groundbreaking psychologists Amos Tversky and Daniel Kahneman, the latter of whom wrote that "I did the best thinking of my life on leisurely walks with Amos." It was the physical activity in the body, Kahneman said, that got his brain going.

When Martin Luther King Jr. was a seminary student at Crozer, he took an hour walk each day through the campus woods to "commune with nature." Walt Whitman and Ulysses S. Grant often bumped into each other on their respective walks around Washington, which cleared their minds and helped them think. Perhaps it was that experience that Whitman was writing about in this verse of "Song of Myself":

> *Know'st thou the joys of pensive thought?*
> *Joys of the free and lonesome heart, the tender, gloomy heart?*
> *Joys of the solitary walk, the spirit bow'd yet proud,*
>   *the suffering and the struggle?*

Freud was known for his speedy walks around Vienna's Ringstrasse after his evening meal. The composer Gustav Mahler spent as much as four hours a day walking, using this time to work through and jot down ideas. Ludwig van Beethoven carried sheet music and a writing utensil with him on his walks for the same reason. Dorothy Day was a lifelong walker, and it was on her strolls along the beach on Staten Island in the 1920s that she first began to feel a strong sense of God in her life and the first flickerings of the awakening that would put her on a path toward sainthood. It's probably not a coincidence that Jesus himself was a walker—a *traveler*—who knew the pleasures and the divineness of putting one foot in front of the other.

How does *walking* get us closer to stillness? Isn't the whole point of what we're talking about to reduce activity, not seek it out? Yes, we are in motion when we walk, but it is not frenzied motion or even conscious motion—it is repetitive, ritualized motion. It is deliberate. It is an exercise in peace.

The Buddhists talk of "walking meditation," or *kinhin,* where the movement after a long session of sitting, particularly movement through a beautiful setting, can unlock a different kind of stillness than traditional meditation. Indeed, forest bathing—and most natural beauty—can only be accomplished by getting out of your house or office or car and trekking out into the woods on foot.

The key to a good walk is to be aware. To be present and open to the experience. Put your phone away. Put the pressing problems of your life away, or rather let them melt away as you move. Look down at your feet. What are they doing? Notice how effortlessly they move. Is it you who's doing that? Or do they just sort of move on their own? Listen to the sound of the leaves crunching underfoot. Feel the ground pushing back against you.

Breathe in. Breathe out. Consider who might have walked this very spot in the centuries before you. Consider the person who paved the asphalt you are standing on. What was going on with them? Where are they now? What did they believe? What problems did they have?

When you feel the tug of your responsibilities or the desire to check in with the outside world, push yourself a bit further. If you're on a path you have trod before, take a sudden turn down a street or up a hill where you haven't been before. Feel the unfamiliarity and the newness of these surroundings, drink in what you have not yet tasted.

Get lost. Be unreachable. Go *slowly*.

It's an affordable luxury available to us all. Even the poorest pauper can go for a nice walk—in a national park or an empty parking lot.

This isn't about burning calories or getting your heart rate up. On the contrary, it's not about anything. It is instead just a manifestation, an embodiment of the concepts of presence, of detachment, of emptying the mind, of noticing and appreciating the beauty of the world around you. Walk away from the thoughts that need to be walked away from; walk toward the ones that have now appeared.

On a good walk, the mind is not completely blank. It can't be—otherwise you might trip over a root or get hit by a car or a bicyclist. The point is not, as in traditional meditation, to push *every* thought or observation from your mind. On the contrary, the whole point is to see what's around you. The mind might be active while you do this, but it is still. It's a different kind of thinking, a healthier kind if you do it right. A study at New Mexico Highlands University has found that the force from our footsteps can increase the supply of blood to the brain. Researchers at Stanford have found that walkers perform better on tests that measure "creative divergent thinking" during and after their walks. A study out of Duke University found a version of what Kierkegaard tried to tell his sister-in-law, that walking could be as effective a treatment for major depression in some patients as medication.

The poet William Wordsworth walked as many as 180,000 miles in his lifetime—an average of six and a half miles a day since he was five years old! He did much of his writing while walking, usually around Grasmere, a lake in the English countryside, or Rydal Water, which is not far from Grasmere. On these long walks, as lines of poetry came to him, Wordsworth would repeat them over and over again, since it might be hours until he had the chance to write them down. Biographers have wondered ever since: Was it the scenery that inspired the images of his poems or was it the movement that jogged the thoughts? Every ordinary person who has ever had a breakthrough on a walk knows that the two forces are equally and magically responsible.

In our own search for beauty and what is good in life, we would do well to head outside and wander around. In an attempt to unlock a deeper part of our consciousness and access a high level of our mind, we would do well to get our body moving and our blood flowing.

Stress and difficulty can knock us down. Sitting at our

computers, we are overwhelmed with information, with emails, with one thing after another. Should we just sit there and absorb it? Should we sit there with the sickness and let it fester? No. Should we get up and throw ourselves into some other project—constructive, like cleaning, or cathartic, like picking a fight? No. We shouldn't do any of that.

We should get walking.

Kierkegaard tells the story of a morning when he was driven from his house in a state of despair and frustration—*illness,* in his words. After an hour and a half, he was finally at peace and nearly back home when he bumped into a friendly gentleman who chattered on about a number of his problems. Isn't that how it always seems to go?

No matter. "There was only one thing left for me to do," Kierkegaard wrote, "instead of going home, to go walking again."

And so must we.

Walk.

Then walk some more.

BUILD A ROUTINE

If a person puts even one measure of effort into
following ritual and the standards of righteousness,
he will get back twice as much.

—XUNZI

Each and every morning, Fred Rogers woke up at 5 a.m. to
spend a quiet hour in reflection and prayer. Then he would
head to the Pittsburgh Athletic Club, where he would swim his
morning laps. As he walked out to the pool he would weigh
himself—it was important that he always weigh 143 pounds—
and as he jumped in, he would sing "Jubilate Deo" to himself. He
emerged from that pool as if baptized anew each day, a friend
wrote, fresh and fully prepared for the workday ahead.

When he got to the set of his television show, the next part of
the ritual began, one that was recorded for posterity in identical
fashion over hundreds of episodes, year after year. The theme
song starts. The yellow light flashes. The camera pans to the

front door. Mr. Rogers enters, singing, and walks down the stairs. He takes off his jacket and neatly hangs it up in the closet. He puts on and zips up his trademark cardigan—the one his mother made him. Then he takes off his shoes and puts on a comfortable pair of boat slippers. Now, and only now, can he begin to speak and teach to his favorite people in the world—the children of his neighborhood.

To some, this might seem monotonous. The same routine, day in and day out, that extended beyond "Cut!" at the end of each show to an afternoon nap, dinner with his family, and a 9:30 bedtime. The same weight. The same food. The same introduction. The same close to the day. Boring? The truth is that a good routine is not only a source of great comfort and stability, it's the platform from which stimulating and fulfilling work is possible.

Routine, done for long enough and done sincerely enough, becomes more than routine. It becomes *ritual*—it becomes sanctified and holy.

Maybe Mr. Rogers isn't your thing. Perhaps, then, you'd rather look at the perennial all-star point guard Russell Westbrook, who begins his own routine *exactly* three hours before tipoff. First, he warms up. Then, one hour before the game, Westbrook visits the arena chapel. Then he eats a peanut butter and jelly sandwich (always buttered wheat bread, toasted, strawberry jelly, Skippy peanut butter, cut diagonally). At exactly six minutes and seventeen seconds before the game starts, he begins the team's final warm-up drill. He has a particular pair of shoes for games, for practice, for road games. Since high school, he's done the same thing after shooting a free throw, walking backward past the three-point line and then forward again to take the next shot. At the practice facility, he has a specific parking space, and he likes to shoot on Practice Court 3. He calls his parents at the same time every day. And on and on.

Sports is filled with stories like Westbrook's. They often feature goalies in hockey, pitchers in baseball, quarterbacks and placekickers in football—the most cerebral positions in their respective games. Players who engage in this kind of behavior are called quirky, and their routines are called superstitions. It's strange to us that these successful people, who are more or less their own boss and are clearly so talented, seem prisoners to the regimentation of their routines. Isn't the whole point of greatness that you're freed from trivial rules and regulations? That you can do whatever you want?

Ah, but the greats know that complete freedom is a nightmare. They know that order is a prerequisite of excellence and that in an unpredictable world, good habits are a safe haven of certainty.

It was Eisenhower who defined freedom as the opportunity for self-discipline. In fact, freedom and power and success *require* self-discipline. Because without it, chaos and complacency move in. Discipline, then, is how we maintain that freedom.

It's also how we get in the right headspace to do our work. The writer and runner Haruki Murakami talks about why he follows the same routine every day. "The repetition itself becomes the important thing," he says, "it's a form of mesmerism. I mesmerize myself to reach a deeper state of mind."

When our thoughts are empty and our body is in its groove, we do our best work.

A routine can be time-based. Jack Dorsey, the founder and CEO of Twitter, gets up at 5 a.m., without fail. The former Navy SEAL Jocko Willink gets up at 4:30 a.m. and posts a picture of his watch to prove it each morning. Queen Victoria woke at 8 a.m., ate breakfast at 10, and met with her ministers from 11 to 11:30. The poet John Milton was up at 4 a.m. to read and contemplate, so that by 7 a.m. he was ready to be "milked" by his writing.

A routine can be focused on order or arrangement. Confucius insisted that his mat be straight or he would not sit. Jim Schlossnagle, the baseball coach who took over TCU's team after a long run of mediocre play, taught his players to keep their lockers, as well as the dugout, spotless and orderly at all times (the team has never had a losing season since and made it to four straight College World Series). The *ordering* also matters to tennis great Rafael Nadal, who drinks water and a recovery drink in the same order and then sets them in a perfect arrangement.

Routine can be built around a tool or a sound or a scent. Rilke had two pens and two kinds of paper on his desk; one was used for writing, while the other was acceptable for bills, letters, and less important documents. Monks are called to meditation by the chiming of a monastery bell; other monks rub a zuko incense on their hands before ceremonies and meditations.

A routine can also be religious or faith-based. Confucius always gave a sacrificial offering before eating, no matter how inconsequential the meal was. The Greeks consulted the Delphic oracle before any major decision and made sacrifices before battle. The Jews have kept the Sabbath for thousands of years, Abad Ha'am once said, just as the Sabbath has kept the Jews.

Done enough times, done with sincerity and feeling, routine becomes ritual. The regularity of it—the daily cadence—creates deep and meaningful experience. To one person, taking care of a horse is a chore. To Simón Bolívar it was a sacred, essential part of his day. When the body is busy with the familiar, the mind can relax. The monotony becomes muscle memory. To deviate seems dangerous, wrong. As if it's inviting failure in.

Some might sneer at this "superstitious" behavior, but that is the wrong way to think about it. As Rafael Nadal explained, "If it were superstition, why would I keep doing the same thing over and over whether I win or lose? It's a way of placing myself in a match, ordering my surroundings to match the order I seek in my head." Did the Greeks really believe that the oracle of Delphi could tell them what they should do? Or was the consultation process, the journey to Mount Parnassus, the whole point?

Sociologists found that island tribes were more prone to create rituals for activities where luck was a factor than where it wasn't, such as fishing on the open sea compared to on a lagoon. The truth is, luck is always in play for us. Luck is always a factor.

The purpose of ritual isn't to win the gods over to our side (though that can't hurt!). It's to settle our bodies (and our minds) down when Fortune is our opponent on the other side of the net.

Most people wake up to face the day as an endless barrage of bewildering and overwhelming choices, one right after another. *What do I wear? What should I eat? What should I do first? What should I do after that? What sort of work should I do? Should I scramble to address this problem or rush to put out this fire?*

Needless to say, this is exhausting. It is a whirlwind of conflicting impulses, incentives, inclinations, and external interruptions. It is no path to stillness and hardly a way to get the best out of yourself.

The psychologist William James spoke about making habits our ally instead of our enemy. That we can build around us a day and a life that is moral and ordered and still—and in so doing, create a kind of bulwark against the chaos of the world and free up the best of ourselves for the work we do.

> For this, we must make automatic and habitual, as early as possible, as many useful actions as we can, and guard against the growing into ways that are likely to be disadvantageous to us, as we should guard against the plague. The more of the details of our daily life we can hand over to the effortless custody of automatism, the more our higher powers of mind will be set free for their own proper work. There is no more miserable human being than one in whom nothing is habitual but indecision, and for whom the lighting of every cigar, the drinking of every cup, the time of rising and going to bed every day,

and the beginning of every bit of work, are subjects of express volitional deliberation.

When we not only automate and routinize the trivial parts of life, but also make automatic good and virtuous decisions, we free up resources to do important and meaningful exploration. We buy room for peace and stillness, and thus make good work and good thoughts accessible and *inevitable*.

To make that possible, you must go now and get your house in order. Get your day scheduled. Limit the interruptions. Limit the number of choices you need to make.

If you can do this, passion and disturbance will give you less trouble. Because it will find itself boxed out.

For inspiration, take as your model Japanese flower arrangers: Orderly. Quiet. Focused. Clean. Fresh. Deliberate. You will not find them trying to practice in noisy coffee shops or bleary-eyed in a rush at 3 a.m. because they planned poorly. You will not find them picking up their trimmers on a whim, or in their underwear while they talk on the phone to an old friend who has just called. All of that is too random, too chaotic for the true master.

A master is in control. A master has a system. A master turns the ordinary into the sacred.

And so must we.

GET RID OF YOUR STUFF

> For property is poverty and fear; only to have
> possessed something and to have let go of it means
> carefree ownership.
>
> —RAINER MARIA RILKE

Epictetus was born a slave but eventually received his freedom. In time, he came to enjoy the trappings of the good life—or at least the Stoic version of it. He had emperors attend his lectures, trained many students, and made a decent living. With his hard-earned money, he bought a nice iron lamp, which he kept burning in a small shrine in his home.

One evening, he heard a noise in the hallway by his front door. Rushing down, he found that a thief had stolen the prized lamp. Like any person who feels attached to their stuff, he was disappointed and surprised and violated. Someone had come into his home and stolen something that belonged to him.

But then Epictetus caught himself. He remembered his teachings.

"Tomorrow, my friend," he said to himself, "you will find an earthenware lamp; for a man can only lose what he has." For the rest of his life, he kept this cheaper earthen lamp instead. Upon his death, an admirer, entirely missing the point of Epictetus's disdain for material items, purchased it for 3,000 drachmas.

One of Seneca's most powerful metaphors is the slaveowner owned by his slaves, or the wealthy man whose vast estates lord over him rather than the other way around (in modern times, we have our own term for this: being "house poor"). Montaigne was perceptive enough to ask whether it was in fact he who was the pet of his cat. We also find a version of it from the East. Xunzi explained:

> The gentleman makes things his servants. The petty man
> is servant to things.

In short, mental and spiritual independence matter little if the things we own in the physical world end up owning us.

The Cynics took this idea the furthest. Diogenes supposedly lived in a barrel and walked around nearly naked. When he saw a child drinking water from a well with his hands, Diogenes smashed his own cup, realizing that he had been carrying around an extraneous possession.

Today, we might call Diogenes a bum or a loser (or a crazy person), and in some sense he was those things. But on the few occasions when Diogenes met Alexander the Great, then the most powerful man in the world, it was Diogenes who observers came away thinking was the more impressive. Because Alexander, as much as he tried, could neither tempt Diogenes with any favors nor deprive him of anything that he had not already willingly tossed aside.

There was nothing but a shirt between the Stoics and the Cynics, joked the poet Juvenal, meaning the Stoics were sensible enough to wear clothes (and refrain from bodily functions in public), unlike the Cynics. This is a pretty reasonable concession. We don't need to get rid of *all* our possessions, but we should constantly question what we own, why we own it, and whether we could do without.

Have you ever seen a house torn down? A lifetime of earning and savings, countless hours of decorating and accumulating until it was arranged just right, the place of so much living—and in the end it is reduced to a couple dumpsters full of debris. Even the incredibly wealthy, even the heads of state showered with gifts throughout their life, would only fill a few more bins.

Yet how many of us collect and acquire as if the metric tonnage of our possessions is a comment on our worth as individuals? Just as every hoarder becomes trapped by their own garbage, so too are we tied down by what we own. Every piece of expensive jewelry comes with an insurance bill, every mansion with a staff of groundskeepers, every investment with obligations and monthly statements to review, every exotic pet and plant with a set of responsibilities. F. Scott Fitzgerald said that the rich are different than us, and his novels portray them as free and without care.

That's not quite right.

Mo' money, mo' problems, and also mo' stuff, less freedom.

John Boyd, a sort of warrior-monk who revolutionized Western military strategy in the latter half of the twentieth century, refused to take checks from defense contractors and deliberately lived in a small condo even as he advised presidents and generals. "If a man can reduce his needs to zero," he said, "he is truly free: there is nothing that can be taken from him and nothing anyone can do to hurt him." To that we would add, "And he or she can also be still."

No one dogged by creditors is free. Living outside your means—as Churchill could attest—is not glamorous. Behind the appearances, it's *exhausting*.

It's also dangerous. The person who is afraid to lose their stuff, who has their identity wrapped up in their things, gives their enemies an opening. They make themselves extra vulnerable to fate.

The playwright Tennessee Williams spoke of luxury as the "wolf at the door." It wasn't the possessions that were the problem, he said, but the dependency. He called it the catastrophe of success, the way that we become less and less able to do things ourselves, the more and more we cannot be without a certain level of service. Not only is all your stuff a mess, but you need to pay someone to come clean it up.

There is also what we can term "comfort creep." We get so used to a certain level of convenience and luxury that it becomes almost inconceivable that we used to live without it. As wealth grows, so does our sense of "normal." But just a few years ago we were fine without this bounty. We had no problem eating ramen or squeezing into a small apartment. But now that we have more, our mind begins to lie to us. *You need this. Be anxious that you might lose it. Protect it. Don't share.*

It's toxic and scary.

Which is why philosophers have always advocated reducing our needs and limiting our possessions. Monks and priests take vows of poverty because it will mean fewer distractions, and more room (literally) for the spiritual pursuit to which they have committed. No one is saying we have to go that far, but the more we own, the more we oversee, the less room we have to move and, ironically, the less still we become.

Start by walking around your house and filling up trash bags and boxes with everything you don't use. Think of it as clearing more room for your mind and your body. Give yourself space. Give your mind a rest. Want to have less to be mad about? Less to covet or be triggered by? Give more away.

The best car is not the one that turns the most heads, but the one you have to worry about the least. The best clothes are the ones that are the most comfortable, that require you to spend the least amount of time shopping—regardless of what the magazines say. The best house for you is the one that feels the most like *home*. Don't use your money to purchase loneliness, or headaches, or status anxiety.

Your grandmother did not give you that brooch so that you would constantly worry about losing it. The artist who produced the painting on your wall was not working hard so that you might one day fear that a guest would damage it. Nor is the memory of that beautiful summer in Anguilla actually contained in that carved statue or the love you share with your spouse limited to the photograph of the two of you at your wedding. The memory is what's important. The experience itself is what matters. You can access that anytime you want, and no thief can ever deprive you of it.

You will hear people say they don't have room for a relationship in their life . . . and they're right. Their stuff is taking up too much space. They're in love with possessions instead of people.

The family who never see each other because the two parents are working late to pay off the extra bedrooms they never use? The fame that keeps someone on the road so much they're a stranger to their kids? The supposed "technology" that is a pain in the ass to figure out, that's always breaking? The fragile, fancy possessions that we're constantly cleaning, buffing, protecting, and trying to find ways to slyly mention in conversation?

This is not a rich life. There is no peace in this.

Take action. Get out from under all your stuff. Get rid of it. Give away what you don't need.

You were born free—free of stuff, free of burden. But since the first time they measured your tiny body for clothes, people have been foisting stuff upon you. And you've been adding links to the pile of chains yourself ever since.

SEEK SOLITUDE

A crowded world thinks that aloneness is always
loneliness and that to seek it is perversion.

—JOHN GRAVES

It was a habit of Leonardo da Vinci's to write little fables to
himself in his notebooks. One tells the story of a good-sized
stone that rested in a pleasant grove, surrounded by flowers,
perched above a busy country road. Despite this peaceful existence, the stone grew restless. "What am I doing among these
herbs?" he asked. "I want to live in the company of my fellow
stones."

Unhappy and alone, the stone contrived to roll itself down
the hill onto the road, where it would be surrounded by countless
other stones. But the change was not quite as wonderful as
expected. Down in the dirt, the stone was trod on by horses,
driven over by wagons, and stepped on by people. It was alternately covered in mud and feces, and chipped at and jostled

and moved—painful moments made all the more painful by the occasional sight the stone was given of its old home, and the solitary peace it had left behind.

Not content to leave the story at that, Leonardo felt the need to put a fine point on it. "This is what happens," he wrote to himself and every one of us, "to those who leave the solitary and contemplative life and choose to live in cities among people full of countless evils."

Of course, Leonardo's biographers were quick to point out that the author didn't always follow the lesson of this fable. He spent most of his life in Florence and Milan and Rome. He painted in a busy studio and attended many spectacles and parties. Even his last years were spent not in secluded retirement but in the bustling court of King Francis I of France.

His occupation required this. As do many of ours.

Which makes cultivating moments of solitude all the more essential. To find solitude, the way Eugen Herrigel said that the Buddhist does, "not in far-off, quiet places; he creates it out of himself, spreads it around him wherever he may be, because he loves it."

While Leonardo was working on *The Last Supper,* he would get up early and arrive at the monastery before any of his assistants or spectators, so he could be alone, in silence, with his thoughts and the mammoth creative challenge in front of him. He was also notorious for leaving his studio and going for long walks by himself, carrying a notebook and simply looking and watching and really seeing what was happening around him. He loved to visit his uncle's farm for inspiration and solitude.

It is difficult to think clearly in rooms filled with other people. It's difficult to understand yourself if you are never by yourself. It's difficult to have much in the way of clarity and insight if your life is a constant party and your home is a construction site.

Sometimes you have to disconnect in order to better connect with yourself and with the people you serve and love.

"If I was to sum up the single biggest problem of senior leadership in the Information Age," four-star Marine Corps general and former secretary of defense James Mattis has said, "it's lack of reflection. Solitude allows you to reflect while others are reacting. We need solitude to refocus on prospective decision-making, rather than just reacting to problems as they arise."

People don't have enough silence in their lives because they don't have enough solitude. And they don't get enough solitude because they don't seek out or cultivate silence. It's a vicious cycle that prevents stillness and reflection, and then stymies good ideas, which are almost always hatched in solitude.

Breakthroughs seem to happen with stunning regularity in the shower or on a long hike. Where don't they happen? Shouting to be heard in a bar. Three hours into a television binge. Nobody realizes just how much they love someone while they're booking back-to back-to-back meetings.

If solitude is the school of genius, as the historian Edward Gibbon put it, then the crowded, busy world is the purgatory of the idiot.

Who isn't stiller in the morning, or when they're up before the house stirs, before the phone rings or the commutes have begun? Who isn't better equipped to notice the meaning of the moment when it's quiet, when your personal space is being respected? In solitude time slows down, and while we might find that speed hard to bear at first, we will ultimately go crazy without this check on the busyness of life and work. And if not driven crazy, we will certainly miss out.

Solitude is not just for hermits, but for healthy, functioning people. Although there is a thing or two we can learn about solitude from the people who turned pro at it.

In 1941, then just twenty-six years old, Thomas Merton reported to the Abbey of Gethsemani in Bardstown, Kentucky, and began his first of many journeys into monkish solitude that would go on, in various forms, for the next twenty-seven years. His solitude was hardly indolent repose. It was instead an active exploration of himself, of religion, of human nature, and later, into solving serious societal problems like inequality, war, and injustice. In his beautiful journals, we find insights into the human experience that would have been impossible if Merton had spent his time in a newspaper bullpen or even on a university campus.

He would come to call solitude his *vocation*. As he wrote:

> To pray and work in the morning and to labor and rest in the afternoon, and to sit still again in meditation in the evening when night falls upon that land and when the silence fills itself with darkness and with stars. This is a true and special vocation. There are few who are willing

to belong completely to such silence, to let it soak into their bones, to breathe nothing but silence, to feed on silence, and to turn the very substance of their life into a living and vigilant silence.

In a more emulatable form of Merton's retreat, Microsoft founder and philanthropist Bill Gates has, twice a year for many years now, taken what he calls a "think week." He spends seven days alone in a cabin in the forest. There, physically removing himself from the daily interruptions of his work, he can really sit down and think.

He might be alone there, but he is hardly lonely. Gates reads—sometimes *hundreds* of papers—quietly for hours at a time, sometimes in print, sometimes off computer monitors that look out over the water. He reads books too, in a library adorned with a portrait of the author Victor Hugo. He writes long memos to people across his organization. The only breaks he takes are a few minutes to play bridge or go for a walk. In those solitary days in that cabin, Gates is the picture of Thomas à Kempis's line *In omnibus requiem quaesivi, et nusquam inveni nisi in angulo cum libro*—"Everywhere I have sought peace and not found it, except in a corner with a book."

Do not mistake this for some kind of vacation. It is hard work—long days, some without sleep. It is wrestling with complex topics, contradictory ideas, and identity-challenging concepts. But despite this struggle, Gates emerges recharged and refocused. He can see further into the distance. He knows what he wants to prioritize, what to assign his people to work on. He carries the quiet stillness of the woods back to the complicated world he has to navigate as a businessman and philanthropic leader.

Each of us needs to put ourselves, physically, in the position to do that kind of deep work. We need to give our bodies, as Virginia Woolf put it, a room of our own—even if only for a few stolen hours—where we can think and have quiet and solitude. Buddha needed seclusion in his search for enlightenment. He had to step away from the world, go off by himself, and sit.

Don't you think you would benefit from that too?

It's hard to make that time. It's hard (and expensive) to get away. We have responsibilities. But they will be better for our temporary disappearance. We will carry back with us the stillness from our solitude in the form of patience, understanding, gratitude, and insight.

In Leonardo's fable, the stone abandoned the peaceful solitude of the meadow for the road and came to regret it. Merton, for his part, came to occasionally regret his complete solitude. Was there more he could do as a man of the world? Could he have a bigger impact if he abandoned his solitude?

Indeed, very few of us are willing or able to make it the totality of our existence, nor should we. (The dancer Twyla Tharp points out that "solitude *without* purpose" is a killer of creativity.) Even in Merton's case, he was given special privileges from his church superior to communicate with the outside world through letters and writing, and eventually began to travel and speak to large crowds. Because his work was too important and the insights he discovered were too essential to remain locked up in a tiny brick house on the edge of the woods in Kentucky.

Merton eventually came to understand that after so much time by himself in the woods, he now possessed solitude inside himself—and could access it anytime he liked. The wise and busy also learn that solitude and stillness are there in pockets, if we look for them. The few minutes before going onstage for a talk or sitting in your hotel room before a meeting. The morning before the rest of the house wakes up. Or late in the evening after the world has gone to sleep.

Grab these moments. Schedule them. Cultivate them.

BE A HUMAN *BEING*

Work is what horses die of. Everybody should know
that.

—ALEKSANDR SOLZHENITSYN

Compared with most royal couples, Queen Victoria and Prince
Consort Albert of Saxe-Coburg and Gotha were excep-
tional. They actually loved each other and they actually worked
at, and took seriously, their jobs as heads of state. This was all
very good.

But it could also be argued that any positive trait—even hard
work—taken to excess becomes a vice.

In both their cases, as a couple for whom, by the nature of
their profession, even the idea of "work/life balance" was impossible, the virtue of their self-discipline and dedication became a fatal vice.

Albert, a Bavarian prince who married into the British royal
family, was a hard worker from the day he married Victoria. He

brought much-needed order and routine to the life of his queen. He streamlined processes and took up a share of the burdens that had previously fallen on Victoria alone. Indeed, many of the so-called Victorian traits of the era originated with him. He was disciplined, fastidious, ambitious, conservative.

Under his pressing, their schedule became one meeting, dispatch, and social event after another. Albert was almost constantly busy, working so much that he occasionally vomited from stress. Never shirking a responsibility or an opportunity, he took on every bit of the burden of power his wife was willing to share, and in turn, together they seized every formal and informal bit of influence the monarchy had in the British Empire at that time. They were a pair of workaholics and proud of it.

As Albert wrote to an advisor, he spent hours a day reading newspapers in German, French, and English. "One can let nothing pass," he said, "without losing the connection and coming in consequence to wrong conclusions." He was right, the stakes were certainly high. For instance, his expert understanding of geopolitics helped Britain avoid being drawn into the U.S. Civil War.

But the truth was, Albert threw himself equally hard into projects of much less importance. Organizing the Great Exhibition of 1851, a nearly six-month-long carnival that showed off the wonders of the British Empire, consumed years of his life. A few days before it opened, he wrote to his stepmother, "I am more dead than alive from overwork." It was, to be certain, a beautiful and memorable event, but his health never recovered.

He was like Winston Churchill, only he and his wife knew no moderation and had little fun. "I go on working at my treadmill, as life seems to me," Albert said. It's not a bad description of the exhausting and repetitive life he and Victoria led. Starting in 1840, Victoria bore nine children in seventeen years, four of whom were born in consecutive years. In a time when women still regularly died during childbirth (anesthesia—chloroform—became available only for her eighth pregnancy), Victoria, who was a mere five feet tall, was constantly pregnant. Even with the benefits of limitless household help, she bore an enormous physical burden on top of her duties as queen. Upon her death, it was found that she was suffering from a prolapsed uterus and a hernia that must have caused her incredible and constant pain.

There's nothing wrong with having a large family—the throne did need heirs—but it never seemed to have occurred to the couple that they had any say in the matter. "Man is a beast of burden," Albert wrote to his brother, "and he is only happy if he has to drag his burden and if he has little free will. My experience teaches me every day to understand the truth of this more and more." As a result, his and Victoria's existence was hardly one of privilege or relaxation or freedom. It was instead an endless cycle of obligation after obligation, done at a breakneck pace that the two of them inflicted on themselves.

It is a testament to their affection for each other that their marriage survived. Victoria was at least aware of the deleterious effects all this work had on Albert. She wrote of the consequences of his "over-love of business" on their relationship, and she also noticed that his health was flagging. His racing mind kept him awake at night, his stomach cramped, and his skin drooped.

Instead of listening to these warning signs, he soldiered on for years, working harder and harder, forcing his body to comply. And then, suddenly, in 1861, it quit on him. His strength failed. He drifted into incoherency, and at 10:50 p.m. on December 14, Albert took his three final breaths and died. The cause? Crohn's disease, exacerbated by extreme stress. He had literally worked his guts out.

Modern medicine has hardly saved us from these tragedies. In Japan they have a word, *karōshi*, which translates to death from overwork. In Korean it's *gwarosa*.

Is that what you want to be? A workhorse that draws its load until it collapses and dies, still shod and in the harness? Is that what you were put on this planet for?

Remember, the main cause of injury for elite athletes is not tripping and falling. It's not collisions. It's overuse. Pitchers and quarterbacks throw out their arms. Basketball players blow out their knees. Others just get tired of the grinding hours and the pressure. Michael Phelps prematurely ended his swimming career due to burnout—despite all the gold medals, he never wanted to get in a pool again. It's hard to blame him either; he'd put everything, including his own sanity and health, second to shaving seconds off his times.

Meanwhile, Eliud Kipchoge, possibly the greatest distance runner ever to live, actively works to make sure he is not *overworking*. In training, he deliberately does not give his full effort, saving that instead for the few times per year when he races. He prefers instead to train at 80 percent of his capacity—on occasion to 90 percent—to maintain and preserve his longevity (and sanity) as an athlete. When Michael Phelps came back to swimming after his breakdown in 2012, it was possible because he was willing to reimagine his approach to training and to approach it with more balance.

Pacing is something athletes are often forced to come to terms with as they age, while young athletes needlessly burn themselves out because they think they have a bottomless well of energy. Yes, there is purity and meaning in giving your best to whatever you do—but life is much more of a marathon than it is a sprint. In a way, this is the distinction between confidence and ego. Can you trust yourself and your abilities enough to keep something in reserve? Can you protect the stillness and the inner peace necessary to win the longer race of life?

It was a malicious lie that the Nazis hung over the gates of Auschwitz: *Arbeit macht frei*—"Work will set you free."*

No. No. No.

The Russian proverb had it better: Work just makes you bent over.

Man is *not* a beast of burden. Yes, we have important duties—to our country, to our coworkers, to provide for our families.

---

*It is worth noting, with dark irony, that Hitler's descent into delirium toward the end of World War II was in many ways brought on by extreme overwork.

Many of us have talents and gifts that are so extraordinary that we owe it to ourselves and the world to express and fulfill them. But we're not going to be able to do that if we're not taking care of ourselves, or if we have stretched ourselves to the breaking point.

The moral of the American tall tale about the rail worker John Henry is often lost on people. He challenges the steam-powered drilling machine, and through sheer strength and in-human will, he beats it. It's great. Inspiring. Except he dies at the end! Of exhaustion! "In real life," George Orwell observed, "it is always the anvil that breaks the hammer."

Work will not set you free. It will kill you if you're not careful.

Prince Albert's children would have gladly traded a less exciting Great Exhibition to have Albert for a little longer, and so too would Queen Victoria and the British people.

The email you think you need so desperately to respond to can wait. Your screenplay does not need to be hurried, and you can even take a break between it and the next one. The only person truly requiring you to spend the night at the office is yourself. It's okay to say no. It's okay to opt out of that phone call or that last-minute trip.

Good decisions are not made by those who are running on empty. What kind of interior life can you have, what kind of thinking can you do, when you're utterly and completely over-worked? It's a vicious cycle: We end up having to work more to fix the errors we made when we would have been better off resting, having consciously said no instead of reflexively saying yes. We end up pushing good people away (and losing relationships) because we're wound so tight and have so little patience.

The bull in Robert Earl Keen's "Front Porch Song" whose "work is never done"? Do you want to be the artist who loses their joy for the process, who has strip-mined their soul in such a way that there is nothing left to draw upon? Burn out or fade away—that was the question in Kurt Cobain's suicide note. How is that even a dilemma?

It's human *being,* not human doing, for a reason.

Moderation. Being present. Knowing your limits.

This is the key. The body that each of us has was a gift. Don't work it to death. Don't burn it out.

Protect the gift.

GO TO SLEEP

There is a time for many words and there is a time for sleep.

—HOMER, *THE ODYSSEY*

A merican Apparel was a billion-dollar company that failed for many reasons. It borrowed too much money. It had a toxic workplace culture. It was besieged by lawsuits. It opened too many stores. This was all written about many times during the company's public disintegration in 2014.

But one cause of its failure—a major reason why more than ten thousand people lost their jobs and a company with $700 million in annual sales simply disappeared—was overlooked by most outside observers.*

When Dov Charney founded American Apparel, he had the notion that he would be a completely accessible boss. As the

---

*It was one I saw firsthand.

company grew from a dorm room operation to a global retailer and one of the largest garment manufacturers in the world, he stuck to that. In fact, his ego swelled at the idea of being at the center of every part of the business.

It was a true open-door policy. Not just open-door but phone and email too. Any employee, at any level of the company, from sleeve sewer to sales associate to photographer, could reach out whenever they had a problem. For good measure, during one of the company's many public relations crises, Charney posted his phone number online for any journalist or customer who had an issue as well.

Early on, this policy had advantages. Charney was constantly in tune with what was happening in the company, and it prevented bureaucracy from establishing itself and bogging people down. But not only did the advantage not scale well, but the costs began to take their toll as well.

You can imagine what happened when the company suddenly had 250 stores in 20 countries. By 2012, Charney was sleeping only a few hours a night. By 2014, he wasn't sleeping at all. How could he? There was always someone with a problem and someone *somewhere in some distant time zone* taking him up on the open-door policy. The human reality of getting older didn't help either.

It was this extreme, cumulative sleep deprivation that was the root of so much of the company's catastrophic failure. How could it not be? Research has shown that as we approach twenty or so hours without sleep, we are as cognitively impaired as a drunk person. Our brains respond more slowly and our judgment is significantly impaired.

In 2014, during a difficult transition between distribution facilities, Charney moved into the shipping and fulfillment warehouse, installing a shower and cot in a small office. To him and some diehard loyalists, this was proof of his heroic dedication to the company. In truth, bad judgment had bungled the transition in the first place, and then his constant presence and micromanaging on site—which became increasingly erratic the longer it went on and the longer he went without sleep—only compounded the difficulties.

Charney descended into madness in front of his employees. Unshaven. Bleary-eyed. At the mercy of his temper, unmoored from even the most basic judgment or propriety. Issuing orders that contradicted orders he had issued just minutes before, he seemed almost hell-bent on destruction. But he was the boss. What could people do?

Eventually, his *mother* was called in to bring him home, to coax him into taking care of himself before it was too late. But he was well past saving. Even back in the normal office, he would call employees late, late into the night and sweetly talk about work until he drifted off, finding that collapsing from exhaustion was the only way he could put himself to bed.

Within a few months of the warehouse episode, Dov Charney was on the verge of losing control of the company. Terms of desperate rounds of financing had made him vulnerable to a takeover, but he agreed to them without thinking through the implications. Sitting before his handpicked board of directors, he mixed package after package of pure Nescafé powder in cold water—essentially mainlining caffeine to stay awake. By the time he left the meeting, he no longer had a job.

Within a few months, his shares of the company were worthless. Investors and debt collectors would find little left to salvage when they sorted through the wreckage. He now owes a hedge fund twenty million dollars and cannot even afford a lawyer.

It was an epic implosion along relatively common lines. The overworked person creates a crisis that they try to solve by working harder. Mistakes are piled upon mistakes by the exhausted, delirious mind. The more they try, the worse it gets and the angrier *they* get that no one appreciates their sacrifice.

People say, "I'll sleep when I'm dead," as they hasten that very death, both literally and figuratively. They trade their health for a few more working hours. They trade the long-term viability of their business or their career before the urgency of some temporal crisis.

If we treat sleep as a luxury, it is the first to go when we get busy. If sleep is what happens only when everything is done, work and others will constantly be impinging on your personal space. You will feel frazzled and put upon, like a machine that people don't take care of and assume will always function.

The philosopher and writer Arthur Schopenhauer used to say that "sleep is the source of all health and energy." He said it better still on a separate occasion: "Sleep is the interest we have to pay on the capital which is called in at death. The higher the interest rate and the more regularly it is paid, the further the date of redemption is postponed."

Arianna Huffington woke up on the floor of her bathroom a few years ago, covered in blood, her head searing with pain. She had passed out from fatigue and broken her cheekbone. Her sister, who was in the apartment at the time, recalls the sickening sound of hearing the body hit the tile. It was a literal wake-up call for both of them. This was no way to live. There was no glamour in working oneself to the bone, trading sleep for an extra conference call or a few minutes on television or a meeting with an important person.

That's not success. It's torture. And no human can endure it for long. Indeed, your mind and soul are incapable of peace when your body is battling for survival, when it is drawing on its reserves for even basic functioning. Happiness? Stillness? Milking the solitude or beauty out of your surroundings? Out of the question for the exhausted, overworked fool.

The bloodshot engineer six Red Bulls deep has no chance of stillness. Nor does the recent grad—or not so recent grad—who still parties like she's in college. Nor does the writer who plans poorly and promises himself he'll finish his book in a sleepless three-day sprint. A 2017 study actually found that lack of sleep increases negative repetitive thinking. Abusing the body leads the mind to abuse itself.

Sleep is the other side of the work we're doing—sleep is the recharging of the internal batteries whose energy stores we recruit in order to do our work. It is a meditative practice. It is stillness. It's the time when we turn *off*. It's built into our biology for a reason.

We have only so much energy for our work, for our relationships, for ourselves. A smart person understands this and guards it carefully. The greats—they protect their sleep because it's where the best state of mind comes from. They say no to things. They turn in when they hit their limits. They don't let the creep of sleep deprivation undermine their judgment. They know there are some people who can function without sleep, but they are also smart and self-aware enough to know that *everyone* functions better when well-rested.

Anders Ericsson, of the classic ten-thousand-hours study, found that master violinists slept eight and a half hours a night on average and took a nap most days. (A friend said of Churchill, "He made in Cuba one discovery which was to prove far more important to his future life than any gain in military experience, the life-giving powers of the siesta.") According to Ericsson, great players nap *more* than lesser ones.

How did the Zen master Hakuin prepare for his epic lecture, *The Records of Old Sokko*? He slept. A lot. He slept so much and so soundly that one of his students said that "his snores reverberated through the house like rumblings of thunder." It went on for more than a month, with Hakuin waking only to see the occasional visitor. But every other minute was spent facedown, passed out in blissful, restful slumber.

His attendants, who had not yet learned to appreciate the power of sleep, began to worry. The day the talks would be given was rapidly approaching. Was the master ever going to get serious about it? Or was he just going to waste his days asleep? They begged him to start working while there was still time. He simply rolled over and slept some more. Finally, as the deadline loomed large, but without a hint of urgency, Hakuin got up. Sitting, he called to his attendants, and began with perfect clarity to dictate the talk.

It was all there. It was brilliant.

It was the product of a rested mind that took care of its body. A healthy soul that could sleep soundly. And it has echoed down through the ages.

If you want peace, there is just one thing to do. If you want to be your best, there is just one thing to do.

Go to sleep.

FIND A HOBBY

> This is the main question, with what activity one's
> leisure is filled.
>
> —ARISTOTLE

William Gladstone, the four-time prime minister of England, in the generation before Winston Churchill, had an unusual hobby. He loved going out into the woods near his home and chopping down trees.

Huge trees. By hand.

In January 1876, he spent two full days working on an elm tree with a girth of some sixteen feet. From Gladstone's diary, we note that on more than one *thousand* occasions he went to the forest with his axe, often bringing his family along and making an outing of it. It was said that he found the process so consuming, he had no time to think of anything but where the next stroke of his axe would fall.

Many critics, one of whom happened to be Churchill's father, criticized Gladstone's hobby as destructive. It really wasn't. Gladstone planted many trees in his life, pruned hundreds more, and aggressively protected the health of the forests near his home, believing that removing dead or decaying trees was a minor but important service. In response to some critics who questioned why he had taken down a particular oak, he explained that removing the rotten members from the forest allowed more light and air to get to the good trees—just as in politics (a joke for which he was promptly cheered). His daughters also sold slivers of wood from the trees their father had cut down as souvenirs to raise money for charity.

But above all, Gladstone's arboreal activity was a way to rest a mind that was often wearied by politics and the stresses of life. During his final three terms as prime minister, from 1880 to the early 1890s, Gladstone was out in the woods inspecting or chopping more than three hundred times. Nor was an axe the only tool he used to relax or be present. Gladstone was also said to enjoy vigorous hikes, and mountain climbing well into old age, and the only thing that appears in his diary more than tree felling is reading. (He collected and read some *twenty-five thousand* books during his life.) These activities were a relief from the pressures of politics, a challenge for which effort was always rewarded and with which his opponents could not interfere.

Without these release valves, who knows if he could have been as good a leader? Without the lessons he learned in those woods—about persistence, about patience, about doing your best, about the importance of momentum and gravity—could he have fought the long and good fight for the causes he believed in?

Nope.

When most of us hear the word "leisure," we think of lounging around and doing nothing. In fact, this is a perversion of a sacred notion. In Greek, "leisure" is rendered as *scholé*—that is, *school*. Leisure historically meant simply freedom from the work needed to survive, freedom *for* intellectual or creative pursuits. It was learning and study and the pursuit of higher things.

As society advanced and jobs became increasingly less physical, but more exhausting mentally and spiritually, it became common for leisure to include a diverse array of activities, from reading to woodwork. Jesus, for instance, rested out on the water, fishing with his disciples. Seneca wrote about how Socrates loved to play with children, how Cato loved to relax with wine, how Scipio was passionate about music. And we know this because Seneca's own leisure from politics was writing thoughtful, philosophical letters to friends. John Cage picked up the hobby of mushroom hunting. He observed that traipsing through the woods opened up the mind and encouraged ideas to "fly into one's head like birds." Fred Rogers had his swimming. Saint Teresa of Ávila loved to dance, and so did Mae Carol Jemison, the first African American woman in space. Simón Bolívar too found dancing a helpful tool in balancing the affairs of state and the burdens of revolution. The writer David Sedaris likes to walk the back roads of his neighborhood in the English countryside and pick up garbage, often for hours at a time. John Graves poured himself into carving out his ranch from the Texas Hill Country, fixing fences, raising cattle, and cultivating the land. Herbert Hoover loved fishing so much, he wrote a book about it. The title: *Fishing for Fun: And to Wash Your Soul.*

The swordsman Musashi, whose work was aggressively and violently physical, took up painting late in life, and observed that each form of art enriched the other. Indeed, flower arranging, calligraphy, and poetry have long been popular with Japanese generals and warriors, a wonderful pairing of opposites—strength and gentleness, stillness and aggression. Hakuin, the Zen master, excelled at painting and calligraphy, producing thousands of works in his lifetime. NBA champion Chris Bosh taught himself how to code. Einstein had his violin, Pythagoras has his lyre. William Osler, the founder of Johns Hopkins University, told aspiring medical students that when chemistry or anatomy distressed their soul, "seek peace in the great pacifier, Shakespeare."

Reading. Boxing. Collecting stamps. Whatever. Let it relax you and give you peace.

In his essay on leisure, Josef Pieper wrote that "the ability to be 'at leisure' is one of the basic powers of the human soul." But that's what's so interesting about it. It's a physical state—a physical *action*—that somehow replenishes and strengthens the soul. Leisure is not the absence of activity, it *is* activity. What is absent is any external justification—you can't do leisure for pay, you can't do it to impress people.

You have to do it *for you.*

But the good news is that leisure can be anything. It can be cutting down trees, or learning another language. Camping or restoring old cars. Writing poetry or knitting. Running marathons, riding horses, or walking the beach with a metal detector. It can be, as it was for Churchill, painting or bricklaying.

Pieper said that leisure was like saying a prayer before bed. It might help you go to sleep—just as leisure might help you get better at your job—but that can't be the point.

Many people find relief in strenuous exercise. Sure, it might make them stronger at work, but that's not why they do it. It's meditative to put the body in motion and direct our mental efforts at conquering our physical limitations. The repetition of a long swim, the challenge of lifting heavy weights, the breathlessness of a sprint—there is a cleansing experience, even if it is accompanied by suffering. It's a wonderful feeling there, right before the sweat breaks, when we can feel ourselves working the stress up from the deep recesses of our soul and our conscious mind and then out of the body.

"If an action tires your body but puts your heart at ease," Xunzi said, "do it." There is a reason philosophers in the West often trained in wrestling and boxing, while philosophers in the East trained in martial arts. These are not easy activities, and if you're not present while you do them, you'll get your ass kicked.

The point isn't to simply fill the hours or distract the mind. Rather, it's to engage a pursuit that simultaneously challenges and relaxes us. Students observed that in his leisure moments, Confucius was "composed and yet fully at ease." (He was also said to be very skilled at "menial" tasks.) That's the idea. It's an opportunity to practice and embody stillness but in another context.

It's in this leisure, Ovid observed, that "we reveal what kind of people we are."

Assembling a puzzle, struggling with a guitar lesson, sitting on a quiet morning in a hunting blind, steadying a rifle or a bow while we wait for a deer, ladling soup in a homeless shelter. Our bodies are busy, but our minds are open. Our hearts too.

Of course, leisure can easily become an escape, but the second that happens it's not leisure anymore. When we take something relaxing and turn it into a compulsion, it's not leisure, because we're no longer *choosing* it.

There is no stillness in that.

While we don't want our leisure to become work, we do have to *work* to make time for them. "For me," Nixon wrote in his memoir, "it is often harder to be away from the job than to be working at it." On the job, we are busy. We are needed. We have power. We are validated. We have conflict and urgency and an endless stream of distractions. Nixon said that the constant grind was "absolutely necessary for superior performance." But was his performance really that superior? Or was that the whole problem?

At leisure, we are with ourselves. We are present. It's us and the fishing pole and the sound of the line going into the water. It's us and the waiting, giving up control. It's us and the flash cards for the language we are learning. It's the humility of being bad at something because we are a beginner, but having the confidence to trust in the process.

No one is making us do this. We can quit if we're struggling, we can cut corners and cheat (ourselves) without fear of repercussion. No money is on the line to motivate us, no rewards or validation but the experience. To do leisure well—to be present, to be open, to be virtuous, to be connected—is hard. We cannot let it turn into a job, into another thing to dominate and to dominate others through.

We must be disciplined about our discipline and moderate in our moderation.

Life is about balance, not about swinging from one pole to the other. Too many people alternate between working and bingeing, on television, on food, on video games, on lying around wondering why they are bored. The chaos of life leads into the chaos of planning a vacation.

Sitting alone with a canvas? A book club? A whole afternoon for cycling? Chopping down trees? Who has the time?

If Churchill had the time, if Gladstone had the time, you have the time.

Won't my work suffer if I step away from it?

Seneca pointed out how readily we take risks with uncertain payoffs in our career—but we're afraid to risk even one minute of time for leisure.

There's nothing to feel guilty about for being idle. It's not reckless. It's an investment. There is nourishment in pursuits that have no purpose—that *is* their purpose.

Leisure is also a reward for the work we do. When we think about the ideal "Renaissance man," we see someone who is active and busy, yes, but also fulfilled and balanced. Getting to know yourself is the luxury of the success you've had. Finding fulfillment and joy in the pursuit of higher things, you've earned it. It's there for you, take it.

Make the time. Build the discipline.

You deserve it. You need it.

Your stillness depends on it.

BEWARE ESCAPISM

> Me miserable! which way shall I fly
> Infinite wrath, and infinite despair?
> Which way I fly is Hell; myself am Hell.
>
> —JOHN MILTON

After the crushing disappointment of the unexpected failure of his great novel *Ask the Dust,* John Fante needed an escape. He would have loved to hit the road, to flee the town and the state that had broken his heart, but he couldn't. Fante was alternately too poor and then too successful as a screenwriter to afford to leave Hollywood. And soon after that, he was too married and had too many kids to support.

Over the years he found many ways to numb the pain he felt. By playing pinball for hours on end (his addiction was extreme enough to be immortalized as a character in William Saroyan's *The Time of Your Life*). By drinking for hours on end in

Hollywood bars, where he kept company with F. Scott Fitzgerald and William Faulkner. By spending so many hours on the course that he turned his ever-patient wife, Joyce, into a golf widow.

It wasn't restoration that Fante was chasing, nor was it leisure, it was *escape* from real life.

In his own words, Fante pissed away decades golfing, reading, and drinking, and by extension *not* writing novels. Because that felt better than getting rejected again and again. Because it was easier than sitting alone by himself in a room, doing battle with the demons that made his writing so beautiful in the first place.

That's the difference between leisure and escapism. It's the intention. Travel is wonderful, but is there not something sad to the story in Johnny Cash's life, as his first marriage fell apart and his music became more formulaic and less fulfilling? Landing in L.A. at the end of a long tour, instead of heading home to his family, he walked up to the counter and asked to buy a ticket. To where? "Wherever the next plane will take me," he told the attendant.

Despair and restlessness go together.

The problem is that you can't flee despair. You can't escape, with your body, problems that exist in your mind and soul. You can't run away from your choices—you can only fix them with better choices.

There's nothing wrong with a good vacation (particularly if the aim is solitude and quiet) or a round of golf, just as there is nothing wrong with cracking a beer to take the edge off. Certainly

Churchill loved to travel and enjoyed champagne, though he stunk at golf.

But too often, the frenzied or the miserable think that an escape—literal or chemical—is a positive good. Sure, the rush of traveling, the thrill of surfing, or the altered state of a psychedelic can relieve some of the tension that's built up in our lives. Maybe you get some pretty pictures out of it, and some pseudo-profundity that impresses your friends.

But when that wears off? What's left?

Nixon watched nearly *five hundred* movies during his time in the White House. We know the darkness he was running from. There's no question that for Tiger Woods, his addictions were in part driven by a desire to escape the pain left over from his childhood. But each time he hopped on a private plane to Vegas instead of opening up to his wife (or to his father while he was still alive), he was setting himself up for more pain down the road. Each time John Fante hit the golf course instead of the keys of his typewriter, or went out drinking instead of being at home, he might have felt a temporary escape, but it came at a very high cost.

When you defer and delay, interest is accumulating. The bill still comes due . . . and it will be even harder to afford then than it will be right now.

The one thing you can't escape in your life is *yourself.*

Anyone who's traveled long enough knows this. It's eventually clear we carry with us on the road more baggage than just our suitcase and our backpacks.

Emerson, who in his own life traveled to England and Italy and France and Malta and Switzerland (as well as extensively across America), pointed out that the people who built the sights and wonders that tourists liked to see didn't do so while they traveled. You can't make something great flitting around. You have to *stick fast,* like an axis of the earth. Those who think they will find solutions to all their problems by traveling far from home, perhaps as they stare at the Colosseum or some enormous moss-covered statue of Buddha, Emerson said, are bringing *ruins to ruins.* Wherever they go, whatever they do, their sad self comes along.

A plane ticket or a pill or some plant medicine is a treadmill, not a shortcut. What you seek will come only if you sit and do the work, if you probe yourself with real self-awareness and patience.

You have to be still enough to discover what's really going on. You have to let the muddy water settle. That can't happen if you're jetting off from one place to another, if you're packing your schedule with every activity you can think of in order to avoid the possibility of having to spend even a moment alone with your own thoughts.

In the fourth century BC, Mengzi spoke of how the Way is near, but people seek it in what is distant. A few generations after that, Marcus Aurelius pointed out that we don't need to "get away from it all." We just need to *look within.* "Nowhere you can go is more peaceful—more free of interruptions," he said, "than your own soul."

The next time we feel the urge to flee, to hit the road or bury ourselves in work or activity, we need to catch ourselves. Don't book a cross-country flight—go for a walk instead. Don't get high—get some solitude, find some quiet. These are far easier, far more accessible, and ultimately far more sustainable strategies for accessing the stillness we were born with. Travel inside your heart and your mind, and let the body stay put. "A quick visit should be enough to ward off all," Marcus wrote, "and send you back ready to face what awaits you."

Tuning out accomplishes nothing. *Tune in.*

If true peace and clarity are what you seek in this life—and by the way, they are what you deserve—know that you will find them nearby and not far away. Stick fast, as Emerson said. Turn *into* yourself. Stand in place.

Stand in front of the mirror. Get to know your front porch.

You were given one body when you were born—don't try to be someone else, somewhere else. Get to know yourself.

Build a life that you don't need to escape from.

ACT BRAVELY

To see people who will notice a need in the world and
do something about it. . . . Those are my heroes.

—FRED ROGERS

In Camus's final novel, *The Fall,* his narrator, Clamence, is
walking alone on a street in Amsterdam when he hears what
sounds like a woman falling into the water. He's not totally certain that's what he heard, but mostly, riding the high of a nice
evening with his mistress, he does not want to be bothered, and
so he continues on.

A respected lawyer with a reputation as a person of great virtue in his community, Clamence returns to his normal life the
following day and attempts to forget the sound he heard. He continues to represent clients and entertain his friends with per-
suasive political arguments, as he always has.

Yet he begins to feel off.

One day, after a triumphant appearance in court arguing for a blind client, Clamence gets the feeling he is being mocked and laughed at by a group of strangers he can't quite locate. Later, approaching a stalled motorist at an intersection, he is unexpectedly insulted and then assaulted. These encounters are unrelated, but they contribute to a weakening of the illusions he has long held about himself.

It is not with an epiphany or from a blow to the head that the monstrous truth of what he has done becomes clear. It is a slow, creeping realization that comes to Clamence that suddenly and irrevocably changes his self-perception: That night on the canal he shrugged off a chance to save someone from committing suicide.

This realization is Clamence's undoing and the central focus of the book. Forced to see the hollowness of his pretensions and the shame of his failings, he unravels. He had believed he was a good man, but when the moment (indeed moments) called for goodness, he slunk off into the night.

It's a thought that haunts him incessantly. As he walks the streets at night, the cry of that woman—the one he ignored so many years ago—never ceases to torment him. It toys with him too, because his only hope of redemption is that he might hear it again in real life and then seize the opportunity to dive in and save someone from the bottom of the canal.

It's too late. He has failed. He will never be at peace again.

The story is fictional, of course, but a deeply incisive one, written not coincidentally in the aftermath of the incredible moral failings of Europe in the Second World War. Camus's message to the reader pierces us like the scream of the woman in Clamence's memory: High-minded thoughts and inner work are one thing, but all that matters is what you *do*. The health of our spiritual ideals depends on what we do with our bodies in moments of truth.

It is worth comparing the agony and torture of Clamence with a more recent example from another French philosopher, Anne Dufourmantelle, who died in 2017, aged fifty-three, rushing into the surf to save two drowning children who were not her own. In her writing, Anne had spoken often of risk—saying that it was impossible to live life without risk and that in fact, *life is risk*. It is in the presence of danger, she once said in an interview, that we are gifted with the "strong incentive for action, dedication, and surpassing oneself."

And when, on the beach in Saint-Tropez, she was faced with a moment of danger and risk, an opportunity to turn away or to *do good,* she committed the full measure of devotion to her ideals.

What is better? To live as a coward or to die a hero? To fall woefully short of what you know to be right or to fall in the line of duty? And which is more natural? To refuse a call from your fellow humans or to dive in bravely and help them when they need you?

Stillness is not an excuse to withdraw from the affairs of the world. Quite the opposite—it's a tool to let you do more good for more people.

Neither the Buddhists nor the Stoics believed in what has come to be called "original sin"—that we are a fallen and flawed and broken species. On the contrary, they believe we were born good. To them, the phrase "Be natural" was the same as "Do the right thing." For Aristotle, virtue wasn't just something contained in the soul—it was how we lived. It was what we did. He called it *eudaimonia:* human flourishing.

A person who makes selfish choices or acts contrary to their conscience will never be at peace. A person who sits back while others suffer or struggle will never feel good, or feel that they are *enough,* no matter how much they accomplish or how impressive their reputation may be.

A person who *does* good regularly will feel good. A person who contributes to their community will feel like they are a part of one. A person who puts their body to good use—volunteering, protecting, serving, *standing up for*—will not need to treat it like an amusement park to get some thrills.

Virtue is not an abstract notion. We are not clearing our minds and separating the essential from the inessential for the purposes of a parlor trick. Nor are we improving ourselves so that we can get richer or more powerful.

We are doing it to live better and *be* better.

Every person we meet and every situation we find ourselves in is an opportunity to prove that.

It's the old Boy Scout motto: "Do a Good Turn Daily."

Some good turns are big, like saving a life or protecting the environment. But good turns can also be small, Scouts are taught, like a thoughtful gesture, mowing a neighbor's lawn, calling 911 when you see something amiss, holding open a door, making friends with a new kid at school. It's the brave who do these things. It's the people who do these things who make the world worth living in.

Marcus Aurelius spoke of moving from one unselfish action to another—"only there," he said, can we find "delight and stillness." In the Bible, Matthew 5:6 says that those who do right will be made full by God. Too many believers seem to think that *belief* is enough. How many people who claim to be of this religion or that one, if caught and investigated, would be found guilty of *living* the tenets of love and charity and selflessness?

Action is what matters.

Pick up the phone and make the call to tell someone what they mean to you. Share your wealth. Run for office. Pick up the trash you see on the ground. Step in when someone is being bullied. Step in even if you're scared, even if you might get hurt. Tell the truth. Maintain your vows, keep your word. Stretch out a hand to someone who has fallen.

Do the *hard* good deeds. "You must do the thing you cannot do," Eleanor Roosevelt said.

It will be scary. It won't always be easy, but know that what is on the other side of goodness is true stillness.

Think of Dorothy Day, and indeed, many other less famous Catholic nuns, who worked themselves to the bone helping other people. While they may have lacked for physical possessions and wealth, they found great comfort in seeing the shelters they had provided, and the self-respect they'd restored for people whom society had cast aside. Let us compare that to the anxiety of the helicopter parents who think of nothing but which pre-school to enroll their toddler in, or the embezzling business partner who is just one audit away from getting caught. Compare that to the nagging insecurity we feel knowing that we are not living the way we should or that we are not doing enough for other people.

If you see fraud, and do not say fraud, the philosopher Nassim Taleb has said, *you are a fraud.* Worse, you will feel like a fraud. And you will never feel proud or happy or confident.

Will we fall short of our own standards? Yes. When this happens, we don't need to whip ourselves, as Clamence did, we must simply let it instruct and teach us, as all injuries do.

That's why twelve-step groups ask their members to be of service as part of their recovery. Not because good deeds can undo the past, but because they help get us out of our heads, and in the process, help us write the script for a better future.

If we want to be good and feel good, we have to *do* good.

There is no escaping this.

Dive in when you hear the cry for help. Reach out when you see the need. Do kindness where you can.

Because you'll have to find a way to live with yourself if you don't.

ON TO THE FINAL ACT

> As a well-spent day brings a happy sleep, so a well-employed life brings a happy death.

> —LEONARDO DA VINCI

It was AD 161 and the emperor Antoninus Pius knew he was going to die. He was seventy-four years old and he could feel the life leaving his body. A fever had taken hold and his stomach pained him. With his last bit of strength, he called his adopted son Marcus Aurelius into the room and began the process of transferring the state over to him. When this task was complete, Antoninus turned to his royal audience and spoke his final word—a word that would echo down through not just the life of his son but all of history, down even to us today: *aequanimitas*.

A few hundred years before, in roughly 400 BC, Buddha accepted with equal equanimity that he too would soon pass from this earth. He was a little older than Antoninus, but he had not certified a successor, for although he was born a prince, he'd renounced his patrimony in the pursuit of enlightenment. Still, he could tell that his students were worried about losing him, about how they would continue their journey without his guidance and love.

"You may be thinking," he said to them, "'The word of the Teacher is now a thing of the past; now we have no more teacher.' But that is not how you should see it. Let the Dhamma and the Discipline that I have taught you be your Teacher when I am gone."

Then, just as Antoninus had done, he prepared for his final words. His last chance for passing on wisdom to the people he loved, to the people he knew would face all the difficulties that life throws at us. "All individual things pass away," he said. "Seek your liberation with diligence."

Then Buddha fell into a deep sleep and never woke again.

It is fitting that between the deaths of these two titans came Epicurus, the philosopher whose unique way of living almost perfectly bridges the Eastern and Western schools. In 270 BC, he also had the self-awareness to know he did not have much more time. "On this happy day, which is the last day of my life," Epicurus began his final letter, "I write the following words to you." Despite the considerable pain he felt, his body racked by blockages in the bladder and bowels, he wrote instead of the joy in his heart, and the fond recollections he had of conversations with his friends. Then he got to the purpose of the letter—a set of instructions for the care of a promising pupil he wanted to make sure was looked after. Within a few hours and without much fanfare, Epicurus would join Buddha and Antoninus in eternity, in death.

Three approaches. Different, but in the end the same.

Clear.

Calm.

Kind.

Still.

Each of the domains we have studied addressed in their own way.

The mind.

The soul.

The body.

The mental. The spiritual. The physical.

Three legs in a stool. Three points along a perfect circle.

None of us are long for this world. Death hangs over us all, whether we notice or not, whether we believe it or not.

Tomorrow, we could discover we have cancer. Two weeks from now, a heavy branch could fall from a tree and take us with it. The prognosis is terminal for each and every person and has been from the moment we were born. Our heart beats without fail for an uncertain amount of time, and then one day, suddenly, it is still.

Memento mori.

This is a fact that, perhaps more than anything else, is

responsible for incredible amounts of anxiety and distress. It's scary to think that we will die. As is the fact that we cannot know for certain what will happen when death comes, whenever that is. Is there such a thing as heaven? Or hell? Is death painful? Is it nothingness, a dark backward abysm of time?

Seneca reminded himself that before we were born we were still and at peace, and so we will be once again after we die. A light loses nothing by being extinguished, he said, it just goes back to how it was before.

The denial of this simple, humbling reality—the denial of death—is why we attempt to build monuments to our own greatness, it's why we worry and argue so much, why we chase pleasure and money and cannot be still while we are alive. It's ironic that we spend so much of our precious time on earth either impotently fighting death or futilely attempting to ignore the thought of it.

It was Cicero who said that to *study philosophy is to learn how to die*.

Most of this book has been about how to live well. But in so doing, it is also about how to die well. Because they are the same thing. Death is where the three domains we have studied in these pages come together.

We must learn to think rationally and clearly about our own fate.

We must find spiritual meaning and goodness while we are alive.

We must treat the vessel we inhabit on this planet well—or we will be forced to abandon it early.

Death brings an end to everything, to our minds, our souls, and our bodies, in a final, permanent stillness.

So we end this book there as well.

AFTERWORD

It's getting to be early evening now, and about time for me to get up from the computer, having made some progress on the pages you just read. Years ago I got myself out of the busy city and set up my family here, on a little spread outside town, with a picture of Oliver Sacks and his "No!" sign hanging above my desk. Now that my writing day is done, I've got work to do on the farm—chickens to feed, some donkeys to sneak carrots to, and fences to inspect. Not unlike the plot of that Zen poem about the taming of the bull, my neighbor's longhorn has gotten onto my property, and I need to go find him.

My young son helps me load some tools into the back of the ATV—"the tractor, the *twahktor*!" he calls it—and then I hug him and head down the levee, through to the middle pasture, and back down by the creek. The fence there has started to weaken, from the elements and the explorations of the wayward bull, and I spend the next hour grabbing and pinching T-post clips. You take the clip and wrap it around the back of the post, grab the end with the pliers, hooking it over the wire and twisting it tight so it can't come loose. Wrap, grab, hook, twist. Wrap, grab, hook, twist.

No thinking, just doing.

The sweat gets going quickly in Texas, and my leather gloves are shades darker almost as soon as I start. But by the end the fence is tight. I tell myself it will hold—or so I hope. Next up is moving the hay, backing the buggy up to the round bale, letting the arm fall over top of it, and then gunning the engine of the ATV. It catches, teeters, flips up, and falls over, two thousand pounds of food now lying flat on the trailer. By the time I've driven to where I need to drop it, the cows have gotten wise to the sound and come running to investigate. I line it up with the hay ring, back up again, and watch it come tumbling off the back. With the knife in my pocket, I cut off the netting and drop the heavy steel hay ring over it to prevent waste. The cows begin to eat, yelling in appreciation, jostling with each other for their place at the bale.

With them properly distracted, it's time for me to go find this bull. I heard him when I was working and suspect he's over in the back corner of the front pasture. I find him there, a ton or more of muscle and horns. I'm a little frustrated. This is not my problem, though my neighbor seems not to mind that this keeps happening. I behold him there, as the poem says, but keep my distance. Not just because I don't want to be gored, but because in rushing this process before, in getting him worked up, I've run the bull right through a barbed-wire fence—a costly reminder of the risks of impatience.

The key is to nudge him in the direction you want to go, to eliminate the other options and then get him moving. It's got to feel like it's his idea. Otherwise, he'll panic and get angry. And the problem goes from bad to worse.

So I just stand there, resting against some cedar, looking up at the first croppings of the Violet Crown—the Texas sunset that settles over Austin—that is coming toward the horizon. In this moment, I am at peace. It doesn't matter how tough things have been lately. It doesn't matter what's going on in the world. My breathing is slowing down. There is no social media here. The outrage factory that has become the news cycle can't reach me. Neither can my clients or business partners—there's no reception in these woods. I am far from this manuscript I have been working on. Far from my research and my notes, from my comfortable office and the craft that I love. And here, far from my work, the story of Shawn Green, which I read months ago, and what he was really teaching us slips from my subconscious into the front of my mind. I get it now. I get what he was after.

Chop wood, carry water. Fix fences, load hay, seize the bull.

My mind is empty. My heart is full. My body is busy.

Attamen tranquillus.

Ryan Holiday

Austin, Texas

WHAT'S NEXT?

Each morning, I write a meditation inspired by Stoic and other ancient philosophy for DailyStoic.com. You can follow along with nearly two hundred thousand other people by signing up at:

DailyStoic.com/email

Or if you'd like some reading recommendations—nourishing, inspiring, challenging books of the sort that wisdom is made from—you can sign up for a monthly list at.

RyanHoliday.net/reading-list

ACKNOWLEDGMENTS

One of the simplest and most accessible entry points into stillness is gratitude. Gratitude for being alive, for the lucky breaks you've gotten, and for all the people in your life who have helped you. Each morning, I try to take some time to think about these very things, but for the most part, such thanks remain private. With this little space allowed to me here, I'd like to thank everyone who helped make this book possible—my wife, Samantha, first and foremost. I am grateful for her guidance and support and natural stillness, which I learn from constantly. My son, Clark, who went on many long walks with me as I worked out the words in this book. My sister, Amy, whose poise and strength as she battles cancer has deeply moved and humbled me. I am grateful to my agent and collaborator, Steve Hanselman, who helped not only with translations but with the shaping of the idea. Nils Parker, who has been a sounding board for my writing ideas for over a decade now, and Brent Underwood for all his help marketing and building my platform. Thank you to Hristo Vassilev for all his important research and fact-checking help.

Niki Papadopoulos, my editor, and the rest of the Portfolio team at Penguin Random House—thank you for all the work on *all* my books. To the *logos* that brought all these people and factors together...

I should also thank my donkeys and cows and goats (for their lessons on *being,* not doing), but there are too many to name. I'm also grateful for the chance to workshop many of the ideas in this book on *Thought Catalog, Observer, Medium,* and DailyStoic.com

My final and most serious gratitude goes out to the thinkers and philosophers whose ideas make up this book. It would not have been possible without them, but more important, their insights and writings have made my life better. I'm grateful too to the heroes (and villains) in the stories written here, as their all-too-human successes and failures both inspire and caution anyone in search of happiness, excellence, and stillness. My own search is nowhere near complete, but their example has helped me make a few inches on a journey that—God(s) willing—is only just beginning.

SOURCES AND BIBLIOGRAPHY

My aim for this book is for it to be as lean and portable as possible. Since there is limited room here and no desire to leave any valuable source out, anyone who wants a bibliography for this book can email:

hello@stillnessisthekey.com

For those looking to do more reading on Eastern or Western philosophy, I recommend the following:

Meditations, by Marcus Aurelius (Modern Library)

Readings in Classical Chinese Philosophy, by Philip J. Ivanhoe and Bryan W. Van Norden (Hackett)

Letters of a Stoic by Seneca (Penguin Classics)

The Bhagavad Gita (Penguin Classics)

The Art of Happiness, by Epicurus (Penguin Classics)

The New Testament: A Translation, by David Bentley Hart (Yale University Press)

Buddha, by Karen Armstrong (Penguin Lives Biographies)

Also by Ryan Holiday

Also by Ryan Holiday and Stephen Hanselman

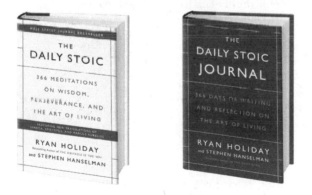

RyanHoliday.net
DailyStoic.com

PORTFOLIO
PENGUIN